The Research Workshop

Dear Paula,

From the very first moment Sarah entered your room, you have been the creator of a journey that has never lost its magic, and has been always inspiring, always extraordinary in extending the boundaries of what is possible.

Your gift for bringing children to the forefront of their awareness, to the part of them that is alive to the world in all its realness and complexity, to the marvel and power that reading and writing can open for them, to the beauty and joy of their learning, to knowing how to teach themselves and each other—all of this and more have not for a moment escaped Sarah and has equally captivated us as parents.

We shall always cherish Sarah's first grade as the beginning of her love for what makes this human drama so intriguing and challenging and for the part we all play in changing, and improving, the "what" and "how" of our lives.

The journey you led us all through will be one we shall never forget—indeed, it will be a beacon for the journeys that are still to be traveled and awakened in each of us.

With much love and gratitude,

Richard Lewis
poet, anthologist, and teacher

Paula brings the world into the classroom, rejoices in its diversity, and the children learn to read and write in the most amazing way. From the beginning, children learn what reading and writing are for through the contribution of their own voices to the world of both children and adults. For me, that's number one. In short, they are so embedded in the FUNCTION of literacy, they never ask the question, "Why would anyone want to read and write?" It is like breathing to them. I know of no other teacher in America who shows so clearly what an education is all about.

—Donald Graves, author of *A Fresh Look at Writing* and *The Energy to Teach*

The Research Workshop

Bringing the World into Your Classroom

Paula Rogovin

HEINEMANN
Portsmouth, NH

Heinemann
A division of Reed Elsevier Inc.
361 Hanover Street
Portsmouth, NH 03801–3912
www.heinemann.com

Offices and agents throughout the world

The author and publisher wish to thank those who have generously given permission to reprint borrowed material:

p. iii: Chelsea Grant's patch about Asadah Kirkland was created for the *People at Work* quilt in Paula Rogovin's class.

Excerpt from "What Can We Do?", words by Sarah Durkee, music by Paul Jacobs. Copyright © 1997. Used by permission of Sarah Durkee.

Excerpt from "SO LONG It's Been Good To Know Yuh (Dusty Old Dust)" words and music by Woody Guthrie. Copyright © 1940, 1950, 1963 by Folkways Music Publishers, Inc., New York. Used by permission of THE RICHMOND ORGANIZATION.

Excerpt from "THIS LAND IS YOUR LAND" words and music by Woody Guthrie. Copyright © 1956, 1958, 1970 by Ludlow Music, Inc., New York. Used by permission of THE RICHMOND ORGANIZATION.

Library of Congress Cataloging-in-Publication Data
Rogovin, Paula.
    The research workshop : bringing the world into your classroom / Paula Rogovin.
        p.   cm.
    Includes bibliographical references and index.
    ISBN 0-325-00370-X (alk. paper)
    1. Education, Elementary—Activity programs—United States—Case studies.   2. Research—Study and teaching (Elementary)—United States—Case studies.   3. Language experience approach in education—United States—Case studies.   4. Education, Elementary—Parent participation—United States—Case studies.   I. Title: Bringing the world into your classroom.   II. Title.

LB1592 .R64 2001
372.13—dc21   2001024573

Editor: Lois Bridges
Production: Elizabeth Valway
Cover design: Jenny Jensen Greenleaf, Greenleaf Illustration & Design
Cover art: Room 407 painting by Andrea Kantrowitz. www.andreakantrowitz.com
Manufacturing: Steve Bernier

Printed in the United States of America on acid-free paper
05 04 03 02 01 RRD 1 2 3 4 5

Contents

Additional research studies are available from Heinemann at www.heinemann.com/ researchworkshop. The topics are:

Research Study: Dance and Dancers

Research Study: Health Care Workers and Scientists

Research Study: Garment Workers

Acknowledgments

People around me know when my class is starting a research study. Besides losing lots of sleep wondering how to begin, where to find resources, how to address certain issues, and where to go for trips, I'm always asking my family, friends, colleagues, and students' families—current and former—for their thoughts.

Every evening when I call my parents, Anne and Milton Rogovin, in Buffalo, they get to hear the ins and outs of our research studies. If you know my parents, you can see their powerful influence on my thinking, feelings, and teaching. If you visit my classroom you'll feel their presence and see their books, news clippings, and even school supplies. You'll see my father's photographs of young dancers in China and of steelworkers and coal miners. If you're wondering where I got my values and my concern for peace and justice and the rights and dignity of workers, look to my parents, whom I love so deeply.

My parents have given these same values to my sister, Ellen Rogovin Hart, and her daughters, Aliya and Malaika, who are also teachers, and to my brother, Mark Rogovin, who is an artist. I thank Ellen, Aliya, Malaika, and Mark and his wife, Michelle, for their love and support.

My sons, David, Steven, and Eric, get to hear about our research studies whether they like it or not, and whether they're at home or away at college. My class knows my sons by their pictures at the entrance to our classroom, and my students always get to hear stories about them. David never misses our Family Celebrations, where he plays his guitar and sings. I love my sons with all my heart. I thank them for their patience while I prepared for school and worked on this book.

I stop every morning in Room 208, Isabel Beaton's room, which everybody passes on the way to here and there at Manhattan New School. Teachers, school aides, paraprofessionals, the principal, and family members all stop to chat. Isabel calls it "chit-chat." Chit-chat is the informal exchange of ideas, information, feelings, and observations about life and teaching that happens in Isabel's room before school, at lunchtime, after school, and in the evening at a cozy restaurant. It's chit-chat you'll hear if you stand in the hallways of MNS, or if you hang out in the schoolyard after school with aunts and uncles, grandparents, parents, babysitters, and others who have come to pick up children. Chit-chat is at the heart of the educational dialogue, and it's where my research studies breed. Thank you, Isabel. And thanks to my colleagues and the families of Manhattan New School for their friendship, support, and participation in that dialogue.

My colleagues: Susan Arias, Joan Backer, Diana Baron, Isabel Beaton, David Besancon, Azzalee Brantley, Ida Mae Chaplin, Regina Chiou, Carmen Colon-Montes de Oca, Dora Cruz, Judy Davis, Elissa Eisen, Doreen Esposito, Jennifer Feinberg, Hillary Fertig, Tara Fishman, Constance Foland, Jordan Forstot, Mindy Gerstenhaber, Eric Heischober, Sharon Hill, Joanne Hindley Salch, Judy Hirsch, Judith Hirschberg, Layne Hudes, Petrana Koutcheva, Judi Klein, Diane Lederman, Rachele Lisi, Patricia Mullines, Amy Mandel, Pam Mayer, Michael Miller, Eve Mutchnick, Kathy Park, Jane Prawda, Denise Rickles, Roberta Pantal Rhodes, Karen Ruzzo, Mary Ann Sacco, Renay Sadis, Lydia Salavarria, Barbara Santella, Pamela Saturday, Gonzalo Serrano, Lorraine Shapiro, Lisa Seigman, James Smith, Sharon Taberski, Kevin Tallat-Kelpsa, Jennifer Vasquez, Michelle Warshaw, Pat Werner, Janet Williams, Debbie Yellin, and Beatrice Zavala.

Shelley Harwayne, our principal, had the wisdom to insist that Isabel be in Room 208 when she first arrived at MNS. Shelley knew that Room 208 was a strategic location. She also knew Isabel, and she anticipated the chit-chat. I can't thank Shelley enough for inviting me to work at MNS in 1994. She brought me into a safe haven where inquiry is welcomed and encouraged. She enabled me to teach to my heart's content. Through this book, I hope to share that experience with others.

Since I wrote this book, Shelley has moved on to become the superintendent of our school district. I want to thank our new principal, Jacqui Getz, also a true believer in inquiry. When I first heard that Jacqui loves social studies, I was delighted.

To the children and families from our class of 1998–99, thank you for bringing happiness to my life and for helping me teach other teachers and families about research studies. You are very important in spreading the word about inquiry teaching. To the family members who helped in the classroom or on trips, sent in resources, came for interviews or arranged them, participated in our many celebrations, helped at quilting bees, helped with Family Homework, and so much more, I truly appreciate what you have done. You are my coworkers: Phoebe Allardice and her parents, Bruce and Vicki; Julie Avellino and her parents, Laura and Anthony; Ashley Beckford and her parents, Jennifer and Eddie; Benjamin Berkowitz and his parents, Steve and Monique; Ruth Brennan and her parents, Carmel and Eugene; Jordan Corbin and his mother, Debbie; Christopher Fox and his parents,

Thomas and Graziella; Aneta Gandalovicova and her parents, Jana and Petr; Romina Giel and her parents, Dvilia and Markus; Chelsea Grant and her parents, Heather and Stephan; Alexandra (Ali) Greenberg and her parents, Robin and George; Simon Guzman and his father, Simon; Samuel Hirscher and his mother, Miriam; Ian-Michael Jablon and his parents, Henrietta and Steve; Paulina Koladzyn and her parents, Jadwiga and William; Dylan Levitt and his parents, Kim and Bruce; Lilli Meier and her parents, Roger and Tricia; Colby Minifie and her parents, Kempy and Bill; Jordan Nassau and his parents, Donna and Richard; Tamiko Orasio and his mother, Diana; Eliana Slurzberg and her mother, Lucy; Annelise Stabenau and her parents, Denise and Jeff; Alexander Stefanov and his parents, Irena and Vlen; Meagan Stromer and her parents, Nicole and Matthew; and Elwin Walker and his mother, Elsa Reece, and his father, Winston Walker (deceased).

You may have read about Dora Cruz in my book *Classroom Interviews: A World of Learning* (1998). Dora first worked in my classroom when her granddaughter, Kathy, was in my class. For three years, Dora worked full time without a salary, helping with reading, math, and research studies; comforting children and giving me insight into their lives; and making copies of our Family Homework and homemade books. Then Shelley grabbed her up to work full time as a paid school aide—one of the best you could ever dream of. I treasure my friendship with Dora, and thank her for all she has done for the children, their families, for Kathy, and me.

If I thanked all of the families from my former classes—people who gave their hearts and souls to the children and whom I consider close friends—the list would be too long to fit on these pages. You know I appreciate you, and I love you.

I love working with student teachers, and appreciate all the hard work mine have done developing research studies, some of which you will read about in this book. I hope that spending time in our classroom has given them a sense of what inquiry teaching can be, and that they will make families part of their curriculum. Thanks to my student teachers who are mentioned in this book: Debbie Ardemendo, Denice Crettol, Karen Dunlop, Amber Frantz, Christine Hayward, Vandelyn Kennedy, Natasha Scott, and Pam Wen.

I want to thank my soul mate and best friend, Mary Trefethen Segall, whom I have known since ninth grade. She and her husband, Seth, have always been there for me. Mary and I do many of the same things in our classrooms, though her students are college freshmen and my are first graders. You can imagine the dialogue we have about teaching.

There are some very special friends I must thank: Becky Berman; Sarah Bob; Lisa Brand; Linda and Lloyd Brown; Naomi, Tom, and Ben Blumenfeld; Vincent Bravetti; Joe Cassidy; Marie, Joe, and John Fuchida; Eileen and Jim Gilbert; David and Rebecca Gopoian; Carol Grocki Lewis; Dawn Harris-Martin; Carol Hutchens; Richard Lewis; Marla Mikelait; Maria, Caesar, Jason, Raquel, and Michelle Munive;

Gail Gordon; Denise, Arthur, and Errol Rubenstein; Ann Sadowsky; Seth Segall; Bertha Small; Minetha Spence; Hallie Wannamaker; and Nancy, Marty, and Gary Willick.

I want to thank the authors, poets, and songwriters whose work we have used in our classroom. You have enriched our research studies and brought joy to our lives.

Many thanks to the heroes—the famous ones, the forgotten ones, and the ones among us in schools, workplaces, and communities around the world—who have worked to make this a better world. You are our inspiration.

I thank Lois Bridges, my editor and friend at Heinemann, who continues to believe in me. We rant and rave at the injustices in the world and in education. Sparks fly in our e-mail when we talk about standardized testing, phonics-only language instruction, and the other ills of our school system. We are of like mind.

Thanks to Barbara Batton; Donald Brand; Ginny Coglin; Esther Cohen; Renee, Paul, Tai, and Kim Chou Mesches; Earl Dotter; Donald Graves; Nora Guthrie; Ivana Espinet of the Teachers College Educational Video Center; Rhetta Maide, my son Eric's English teacher at Teaneck High School; Brian Pinkney; Robbie Simpson; Vera B. Williams, and the management and workers at the Kraft Hat Factory in the Bronx.

My class interviewed these people during the 1998–99 school year as part of our research studies:

Barbara Abrash	Sarah Durkee	Jordan Nassau's aunt,
Kim Anderson	Jana Gandalovicova	Clorinda
Anthony Avellino	Stephan Grant	Raymond Oberdecker
Phil Batton	George Greenberg	Alicia Perez
Steve Berkowitz	Robin Greenberg	Crescinciana Perez
Monique Berkowitz	Nora Guthrie	Jimmy O'Sullivan
Becky Berman	David Herscher	Sheila O'Sullivan
Carmel Brennan	Miriam Herscher	Eddie Pizarro
Fred Cannizzaro	Judy Hirschberg	Jodi Schulson
Sharon Carpenter	Henrietta Ho-Asjoe	Robert Snyder
Tony Chang	Paul Jacobs	Irena Stefanov
Leonora Colbert	Asadah Kirkland	Nicole Stromer
Jennifer Crowl	Jadwiga Koladzyn	Evelyn Sucher
Dora Cruz	William Koladzyn	Ed Vargas
Brenda Davis	Bruce Lane	Priscilla Wilson
Bobby De Cola	Luberta Mays	

Their impact on our lives was tremendous. The issues they raised, the things they taught us, and the values that shone through as they answered our questions will live in our hearts.

Introduction

Several years ago, a student teacher I'll call Jane came into class early one morning with plans for her research group mapped out for a month. Jane was a competent and hardworking young woman who was coming to teaching after several years in the business world. She had planned a fine series of activities and printed them in calendar format. I had asked my student teachers to write down their plans, and here were Jane's.

Jane thought I would be delighted. I told her that I was pleased that she had put so much effort into her planning, and I was. However, the lack of expression on my face told her there was a problem. I tried to explain; I even called Jane at home that night because I could sense she was hurt by my response. A plan such as this one, all packaged in a plastic cover, would have gotten an A+ at her former job.

Why did my heart drop when I saw Jane's plans? Because they reminded me of my own elementary school education and the curriculum guides, basal readers, pacing calendars, and calendar-like plan books I was required to use during my first twenty years of teaching. That was before my arrival six years ago at Manhattan New School, known also as MNS and P.S. 290, a public school in District Two in New York City.

Jane's plans, like the curriculum guides of old, had a good list of activities and concepts to be developed. That's important. There must be short- and long-term planning—they're essential. There should be some guidelines and standards. I'm in favor of them.

What was missing were the children and their families. How could I explain that to Jane in the half-hour before the children would enter the room that day? I couldn't, really. It would take the whole semester, and then some. It has taken me years of teaching in two different kinds of settings and years of working with other educators, reading, studying, and challenging myself, to become an educator in an inquiry-based, family-involved classroom.

Research studies are not neat. It's easy to say, "step one, step two, step three," as in a curriculum guide, but that doesn't work for a research study. There are too many twists and turns and too many strands that just won't fit in the calendar format of a plan book.

When several teachers and principals from Sweden sat in my classroom recently, they pointed out to me the similarity of what they observed to what the Reggio Emilia schools in Northern Italy do. I rushed to get a copy of *The Hundred Languages of Children: The Reggio Emilia Approach—Advanced Reflections* (Edwards, Gandini & Forman 1998). I was stunned by the similarity of vision and couldn't put the book down. I filled it with underlined passages, enthusiastic marginal comments, and stars meaning "Oh, yes!"

Loris Malaguzzi, one of the founders of the Reggio Emilia schools, commented

No, our schools have not had, nor do they have, a planned curriculum with units and sub-units (lesson plans), as the behaviorists would like. These would push our schools toward teaching without learning. We would humiliate the schools and the children by entrusting them to forms, dittos, and handbooks of which publishers are generous distributors.

Instead, every year each school delineates a series of related projects, some short range and some long. These themes serve as the main structural supports, but then it is up to the children, the course of events, and the teachers to determine whether the building turns out to be a hut on stilts or an apartment house or whatever. (86–87)

Reading about the Reggio Emilia schools gave me a window into my own teaching and prompted me to examine my work more closely—a healthy thing for every teacher. I asked questions of myself, acquired names for practices for which I had no names, and tried new practices. I am still learning.

MNS is a neighborhood school where inquiry flourishes. Principal Shelley Harwayne established the school with a number of visionaries in 1992. You can read about MNS in three books by Shelley. (See the bibliography.) I joined the faculty in 1994. The school abounds with literature (purchased with funds that in many schools would have been used for basal readers). The classrooms and halls, painted beautiful shades of lavender, blue, green, and yellow, are filled with the children's art and writing. There's continuity between the grades because we have common goals for the children. There's even a book club for teachers. Every Wednesday we meet for two hours after school to discuss issues such as how to help our struggling readers or how to enhance our read-alouds—truly an inquiry approach to staff development.

The classrooms at MNS are different, and their differences are valued. Family members are welcome in the school. Parents and grandparents read with children, answer interview questions, paint murals, attend planning meetings, help in the lunchroom, and work on PTA projects.

It was a pleasure to watch Jane's thinking and teaching evolve as she opened the doors to inquiry. She learned to throw questions back to the children, challenging them to find the answers instead of giving them the answers. She talked with the families in the schoolyard and thought of ways to bring their worlds into the classroom. Her written plans put the children and their families in clear focus. When Jane completed her student teaching, we hugged as she said, "I think I understand now. Thank you."

Can This Happen in Any Classroom?

Any teacher can develop an inquiry classroom. Inquiry is a way of teaching and learning, a process that can happen whether you work with the whole class or with smaller research groups, whether or not you have student teachers or others to help.

What's Ahead in This Book?

This book gives you a look inside an inquiry classroom: my 1998–1999 first-grade class at Manhattan New School. It looks at what's missing from traditional curriculum guides and pacing calendars—the children and their families—and describes how to make them the foundation of your planning and curriculum.

The first six chapters lay out the foundation for inquiry and guided research:

- What is inquiry teaching?
- What is guided research?
- How can we involve families?
- How is the classroom organized for guided research?
- What are some of the specifics of writing in an inquiry classroom?
- What are some of the specifics of reading and literature in an inquiry classroom?

Chapters 7 and 8 are about two actual research studies: People Who Make or Drive Vehicles and Woody Guthrie. Three more research studies are available on the web at www.heinemann.com/researchworkshop.

As you read about the research studies, you will see the sequence of activities and events over time. It would be so much easier for the reader if I just wrote about the Research Workshops, one after the other. But, because the work was interdisciplinary, it is important to look at the Research Workshops and the related work at Reading Workshop, Math Workshop, Meeting, and Center Time. It's important to look at the interviews and the trips we had to see how they enhanced the learning. And I want you to see the thinking behind my planning.

As you read about the research studies, you will see the many strands that became the fabric of the research. There are several headings that facilitate looking at the different aspects of our guided research:

Research Workshop   This section tells about the specific activities at the daily Research Workshop.

Share Time   Sharing is a vital aspect of our research studies. This section describes what happens during Share Time and shows the many ways we share information in the classroom and the community.

Planning   This section describes our planning: how we involved families, how guided research became interdisciplinary, how we raised gender issues, and how we strove to make the work multicultural.

Reflecting on the Teaching   This section lets you can take a look at my thinking and my philosophy about an issue. You may find my ideas both thought-provoking and controversial. This section could be a good starting point for discussions.

Family Involvement   Here you will find a multitude of ways to build family involvement into your teaching, and you will see reasons for families to participate in the learning experience.

Interview   Interviews are vital to our research, so there are descriptions of many of the interviews we did.

Family Homework   As you watch the research unfold, you will see the ongoing communication with the families in excerpts from the Family Homework. These excepts are relevant to the two research studies in this book and the three research studies on the web.

Extending the Research—Because our research is interdisciplinary, there are special headings to show how it was extended through the various curriculum areas:

Extending the Research into Reading Workshop
Extending the Research into Math Workshop
Extending the Research into Writing Workshop
Extending the Research into Center Time

Extending the Research Outside of the Classroom: A Trip   When we couldn't bring the world into our classroom, we ventured out beyond our school. This section describes our numerous trips.

Social Action   This section includes numerous examples of social action as it evolved from the research studies.

Summary   At the end of each of the research studies, there is a summary of these aspects of the study:

- Interdisciplinary Aspects
  Writing
  Reading
  Literature
  Art
  Music and Dance
  Science and Health Science
  Math
  Drama
  Social Studies
- Multicultural Aspects
- Gender Issues
- Family Involvement
- Resources Used

The world of an inquiry classroom is filled with surprises. Please come into our classroom and watch as our research studies unfold.

1

Inquiry

What Is Inquiry?

Babies are inquisitive little people. They climb all sorts of things to find out what's up there—even when they risk falling. They wonder as they crawl to all sorts of places. "How can I get out of this crib?" They experiment: "Will these blocks balance?" They try again and again.

Even before they have language, babies experiment to find the easiest way to get some ice cream. If I cry, will I get the ice cream? When they push the food off the high chair, we can just imagine them asking, "Why do I have to eat that? I don't like it." or saying, "I'm not hungry any more." They cry at bedtime, and they're probably asking a perfectly reasonable question: "Everyone else is still up. Why do I have to go to sleep?"

As babies learn to speak, they ask "Why this?" "Why that?" "What is this?" "How come?" "When will we get there?" "Why is the sky blue?"

Experimenting, asking questions, and finding answers is inquiry. It is research. Inquiry is a way of learning.

The same process of inquiry can continue in the classroom. In an inquiry classroom, children's interests and questions become the central focus of the curriculum. Inquiry can enable all children to fully develop their minds and to go into territory previously closed to young people.

Formal Research for Young Children?

What a joyous scene the inquiry classroom is! You hear the hum of young children deeply engaged in research. Even children who are usually restless and unfocused get drawn in to research studies. Formal research studies can be lots of fun. Fun in school? Yes: There can be joy in inquiry. It's empowering to ask questions and find answers. And it's fun to learn about all sorts of other issues and topics as you look for answers to your questions.

Understanding is developmental. Just as babies do, school-age children work at understanding the world around them. Formal research studies are a continuation of the informal inquiry we do in the earliest years of our lives—and they approximate the research done by some adults.

Our understanding of the world deepens when we inquire and investigate throughout our lives. Promoting inquiry in classrooms helps children develop into questioning and thinking adults. Inquiry is a lifelong process. An inquiry classroom is a place where children plant the seeds and adults provide nourishment, sunlight, and water to help them grow.

Here is an example: When my first graders did research about Vincent Van Gogh with student teacher Christine Hayward, they looked closely at a number of his paintings. They observed the dots, dabs, and lines; the multitude of colors representing a single object. They took notes in their journals and made their own pictures imitating Van Gogh's techniques. They even painted a mural called *Starry Night*. In response to someone's comment that he was "crazy," the children took time to discuss brain disorders in a first-grade way and to find more appropriate words to use when talking about brain disorders.

Did they know Vincent Van Gogh? A little. More than enough for Chelsea Grant to write this wonderful poem, which hung in the classroom with the mural:

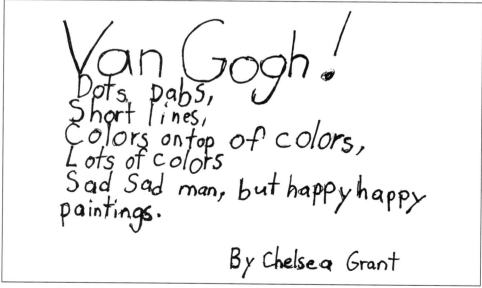

Figure 1–1. "Van Gogh," a poem by Chelsea Grant.

How much did the children know Van Gogh? There's so much to know—do we adults know him? After several weeks of research, the children had some information. But what was more valuable than the particular facts were the concepts and issues that came up in the process of gathering the facts.

I'm sure the children could talk about Van Gogh's style. They probably remember looking at the dots, dabs, and lines that gave the impression of water, flowers, and people. They may remember making their *Starry Night* mural. They could probably tell you that Van Gogh had a brain disorder that made his life very difficult, and they might even talk about Van Gogh in relation to someone they know who suffers from mental illness.

Many of the children will have a lifelong interest in Van Gogh. When they see a copy of one of his paintings on a billboard or at the doctor's office, many will think back to their research and make a comment about it—a comment that may lead to a conversation.

In the middle of a rehearsal for our end-of-the-year play, someone turned to look at a Faith Ringgold poster on the wall behind the stage. One child showed another and the rehearsal stopped when the children shouted, "Paula, there's a picture of Van Gogh in the poster!" It was his self-portrait. The children were delighted with themselves, and I was willing for the rehearsal to stop so we could rejoice in their finding.

Within days of my writing the previous paragraph, Chelsea's grandmother, Dawn Harris-Martin, called long-distance from her vacation spot just to tell me that Chelsea had been watching TV when she saw something about Van Gogh. Chelsea screamed and ran to tell Dawn. She was so excited, it was as if she were a close friend of Van Gogh's. Dawn and I talked about the impact of our classroom research. She said that it has become part of Chelsea's life and always will be. Every time Chelsea sees or hears anything related to last year's research, she is energized. Even her younger sister perks up because she was there when Chelsea did the Family Homework for the Van Gogh inquiry study.

Why Let Children in on the Decision Making?

Why should we let children in on classroom decision making, traditionally left to adults? When children help make decisions about their topics of inquiry, they feel important—they are empowered. They might think, "Wow, I said that I was interested in learning about people who make cars, and the teacher listened to me. We did research about that for three months." When I was a child, my questions weren't welcome in the classroom. I yearn to hear my students' questions and to let their voices guide my planning.

In an inquiry classroom, we must always seek a balance between the required curriculum, the standards, our own interests, the interests of the families, and the interests of the children for whom we work so hard. What do they want to learn about? What is of interest to them?

Did you enjoy reading about Dick and Jane (if you are of that generation)? I absolutely hated reading about their suburban life day after day, about Dick and Jane and then Ted and Sally, who looked like white children with brown faces. That is why I yearn to let the children see others like themselves, families with different backgrounds, and workers other than the traditional policemen, firemen, and mailmen. I yearn to empower them to follow their own interests and expand their worlds.

How Can Teachers Promote Inquiry?

Children need to know that their questions, comments, and observations are welcome in your classroom. These things feed the classroom dialogue, and from them evolve meaning and knowledge.

My students know that I absolutely love for them to ask questions and make comments or observations at any time, anywhere. How do they know that? Why do they feel so comfortable?

- I compliment the children nearly every time they ask a question or make an observation:

    "Wow, great question."
    "That's an amazing observation. Would you say that again for the whole class?"
    "What a great thinker you are."
    "I'm so glad you asked that question."
    "That's a tough question. Now we really have to work to find the answer."
    "You know, I want to write that down. What a terrific observation."
    "Unbelievable. I'm gonna call your mother. I must tell her. What a great observation."
    "You're a smart cookie."

You may think this sounds silly—but it doesn't to a kindergartner or first grader. They eat it up. Besides making a particular child feel terrific, compliments set a chain reaction in motion: The other children want to hear you compliment them, too, so they start asking questions and making observations.

- I forbid children from making fun of other people's questions. The children know that they will never be ridiculed for their ideas in our classroom.
- I give each child time to process information and to speak uninterrupted, explaining to the other children that I value everyone's opinion. This includes children who process information slowly, stutter, or are extremely shy. We wait, and while we wait, the other children's hands must be down.
- We try to deal with each question or comment:

  "Yes, we'll have to think about that during Research Workshop."

  "Great question, boys and girls, what do you think about that?"

  "Perhaps we can ask someone for help with that question. Who can we ask?"

  "We won't have time to deal with your question now, but let's write it down and we'll find a time to deal with it."

  "Great question—how are we going to find the answer to that?" (Take suggestions.)

  "Great question. Maybe you can ask your family to help you answer that." (For a question about religion.)

  During and at the end of a formal research study we assess whether we have answered all the questions. If we haven't, we acknowledge that.
- I tell the principal, teachers, custodian, school aide, and visitors about children's great observations and thoughtful questions.
- I tell the families that I love for their children to ask questions. I encourage them to let their children ask questions and make observations at home, too. You can see how I do this in the Family Homework from the first week of school in September (see Appendix). In addition, we discuss this at family meetings.

Here is an example from our research study about garment workers. The class interviewed Ed Vargas, a parent at Manhattan New School and an organizer for UNITE, the Union of Needletrades Industrial and Textile Employees. Jordan Nassau had just twisted around to look at the label on his T-shirt, and he could hardly wait to ask a question: "How could my Yankees shirt be made in a factory in Mexico? The Yankees are from New York City. Mexico is far away. That doesn't make sense. It should be made in a New York City factory." I elevated Jordan to great heights: "What a brilliant question, Jordan. Eddie, isn't that an incredible question?" Ed agreed. Jordan was delighted.

We used the next twenty minutes of the interview to role-play an answer to Jordan's question. All the rest of the year, I brought up the fact that Jordan had asked a great question that had helped the whole class understand the issue of sweatshop

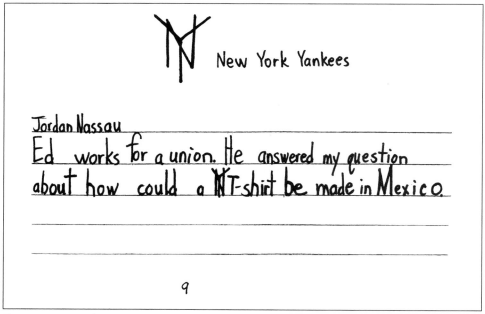

Figure 1–2. Jordan Nassau's page from our homemade book *Ed Works for a Union, Our Interview of Ed Vargas, Who Works for UNITE*. April.

labor. I told his parents, visitors, and Jordan's Aunt Clorinda when she visited from Pittsburgh. Jordan had entered the class with low self-esteem. He continued to ask questions and to make brilliant observations the whole year. His self-esteem soared, and his parents and I were thrilled.

Children learn very quickly whether their questions will be welcomed. When you silence their questions, after a while the children take their minds out of questioning mode. Loris Malaguzzi said

> Once children are helped to perceive themselves as authors or inventors, once they are helped to discover the pleasure of inquiry, their motivation and interest explode. They come to expect discrepancies and surprises . . . To disappoint the children deprives them of possibilities that no exhortation can arouse in later years. (Edwards, Gandini & Forman 1998, 68)

How Can We Promote Participation?

It's important for a teacher to look at the dynamics of a class, to see who is participating and who isn't, then to think about how to change the dynamic. Here are some of my classroom rituals for encouraging full and democratic participation:

- Let children talk in groups of two or three first, before they talk in front of the whole class. I often say, "Turn to the person next to you and talk about this." Several minutes later, we have our whole-class discussion. This gives everyone—not just the three or four children the teacher may call on—an opportunity to speak. Children for whom English is a second language hear other children talking, which may help them formulate their own thoughts. Children who are reticent feel more comfortable participating in small groups.

- Model these small-group discussions: Bring a child over to you and pretend you are partners. At first, don't listen to or even look at each other—stare at the ceiling instead. The children may laugh at your antisocial behavior. Let the class explain why you, their teacher, are not being a good partner. Role-play the scene again, this time being a good partner by looking at your partner and focusing on what she is saying.

- Have students raise their hands rather than call out. This can help prevent children from getting locked out of the discussion by other children who tend to dominate.

- Call on children whether or not they raise their hands. If the child you call on doesn't have a question or comment, say that you will be coming back in a few minutes for their thoughts.

- Have children put their hands down when another child is speaking so that child will not feel pressure.

- To help children who are reluctant to speak, tell them beforehand that you want to call on them during the discussion. Talk about this privately with a child before a class discussion. Then they will think more actively.

- Give each child as much time as possible. Some children process more slowly and need a few extra seconds to formulate their questions or comments. Refrain from completing a child's sentence.

- Celebrate breakthroughs. When a child finally starts to participate, to read, or to write—even just a little bit—celebrate. Compliment that child privately or in front of the class. Ask for comments from the other children. There are always a few children who will make statements that are so complimentary you just want to hug them. That kind of support will encourage even greater participation from the children.

Why Do We Need the Participation of the Children's Families?

Classroom teachers are not the only educators of our children. Their primary teachers are their families, and there are other teachers along the way—neighbors, friends, storekeepers, workers at the local construction site, building superintendents, crossing guards, TV, movies, billboards, and more. There are even a number of *miseducators*—substance abuse, crime, commercialism, and so on. Not only do we have to help the children move in a positive direction, we must also combat the negative influences in our society.

Teachers need not see ourselves as the solo pilot on the airplane. Each of us has limited life experience. Our students' families, extended families, and community must be our coworkers. With all of their life experiences, various perspectives, knowledge, and observations, students' families bring a richness and fullness to the classroom that cannot come from a solo teacher.

We cannot overlook the importance of family involvement in the process of inquiry. It's tough for a child to ask questions in school only to be told at home to be quiet and watch TV. If families have long ago, perhaps inadvertently, stifled the inquiry process, we can encourage them to bring it back into their family life. If families do promote inquiry, we can help make it even more effective. I have seen many, many families who have started to encourage questions at home and who have joined in the search for answers.

The big question is, how can we involve families in their children's classroom experience? How do we involve working parents, parents who juggle work and their own studies, single parents who struggle to keep things together, families who don't know English, and families who strive to survive economically? As you read this book, you will see that there are multiple answers to that question.

I want all of my students to have equal access to learning. I have found that this can be done most fully when their learning experience is shared with their families. Students' learning is enriched through a partnership with families. The world becomes our classroom.

2

Guided Research—What Is It?

What Is an Inquiry Classroom?

William Butler Yeats, the Irish poet and dramatist, said that education is not filling a pail, but "lighting a fire."

Inquiry is our curriculum and our way of life. It is asking questions, searching for answers, and finding multiple ways to find answers. Inquiry can be joyous. It brings the world into our classroom, and the world—so full and so rich, so complex and so simple—makes teaching and learning in an inquiry classroom an adventure.

During guided reading or during minilessons before Writing Workshop, we develop strategies for reading and writing. During guided research we develop strategies for doing research. The model described in this book works in my first-grade class. It can't and shouldn't be replicated, because each classroom is so different, but you are welcome to adapt the basic concepts or any of the actual research studies for your class.

The excerpts from Family Homework in the Appendix show many details about our guided research and how I tried to explain the concept and process to the class families.

Who Determines the Research Study Topic?

Inquiry is a way of learning, not a topic. A research study needs a topic or a theme to focus on. You may be in a school where you are required by the board of education, the principal, or the board of directors to teach certain topics in each curriculum area. Sometimes the requirements are detailed and specific, and leave little room for an inquiry approach. Perhaps you are in a school where teachers can determine their own topics. Whether you must work with required topics or can make your own choices, you can create an inquiry classroom.

Setting the Topic

Teachers who have a required topic can push its boundaries to broaden its scope. My colleague Isabel Beaton says that when you have a mandated topic that you want to stretch, "you teach between the cracks." For teachers who can set their own topics, it is important to select a topic that is broad. Whether we have to push the boundaries of a required topic or can set our own, we must leave plenty of room for the interests of the children, their families, and ourselves. Topics must be broad enough to be broken into subtopics that interest specific children, and there must be enough potential resources to sustain the children's research. The goal is to create a content-rich classroom. Children will connect to a topic if there is something in it for them.

Here are some early childhood social studies topics that are broad enough to be divided into subtopics for research studies:

People at work
Where are our families from?
Our families
Our families at work
People at work in our neighborhood
Who are the people in our neighborhood?
Immigration, and migration within the U.S.
Housing (can include homelessness)
Where do we get our food?
Our town or city
Our block (or another specific block)
Who works in our school?
Early Native American life
Where we live now

Proposing Subtopics

The first day of school, we had a class discussion about our theme, People at Work. Then I asked the children, "Which jobs do you want to learn about?" We made a list:

dancers
artists
people who make cars, trucks, trains, motorcycles . . . (we added the word *vehicles*)
people who drive vehicles
singers

people who take care of our health
baseball players, soccer players . . . (we added the word *athletes*)

My student teachers and I sat down later that day to narrow the list to three subtopics: people who make or drive vehicles (which would enable us to include Chelsea's father, a subway train operator), athletes, and dancers. Since I had students teachers, we would form a research group around each subtopic. In the years I had no student teachers, I worked with the whole class on one subtopic at a time.

One year we worked as a whole class for six months. Our topic was a particular block on Second Avenue near MNS. Our subtopics were the questions the children had asked: Who works on our block? Who lives on our block? What was it like on our block a long time ago? What was it like a long, long, long time ago? Who built the buildings and how were they built? What signs are on our block? We worked with each subtopic from one week to two months.

Thinking About Gender and Diversity

Whether our school is diverse or not, if teachers think about diversity and gender we can make our research studies reflect that concern. This should be done from the start, not as an add-on. If, for example, the topic is People at Work, we can research jobs from which women or minorities have been excluded in the past or from which they are still excluded. These include firefighters, construction workers, miners, doctors, pilots, bus drivers, subway train operators, and more. Bessie Coleman was excluded from studying to be a pilot in the United States not only because she was a woman, but also because she was black. If you do a research study about pilots, consider learning about Bessie Coleman. When children do research about people who drive subway trains, find ways to raise the issue of exclusion of minorities and women from that job.

Should We Work in Small Groups or with the Whole Class?

Sometimes I choose to do a research study with the whole class; sometimes, in small groups. Young children usually need an adult presence, particularly in the beginning of the year. Once children can read fluently, groups can function more easily without the constant presence of an adult. Groups of four to ten children are ideal. Each child can become an active participant. I sometimes divide the class into two groups. Group work can be facilitated by involving family members, student teachers, school aides, and paraprofessionals, or by having groups work independently while the teacher rotates among them. On days when a student teacher or volunteer is not there, the children in that person's group may join my research group.

Deciding Who Will Be in a Research Group

Generally, children can choose which group they will join. When too many children volunteer for a particular group, I use all my powers of persuasion to get some of them to switch groups. I sometimes decide who will be in which group. For example, if one group has too many children with poor self-control and an adult who may not be able to handle them, I will move one of the children to another group. Some children need to be in my group because I can provide the structure they need. As they learn to focus and work better with other children, I give them greater freedom of choice.

The delightful thing about our research groups is that they are usually heterogeneous: They have a mix of genders, cultural and racial backgrounds, and abilities. Getting a mix of genders is sometimes difficult, but there are ways to help. For example, when only girls want to join a dance research group, I show the children pictures of male and female dancers. When a boy volunteers to join the group, freeing himself from social pressures, I give him a great compliment. That praise usually encourages a second boy to join. If a vehicle research group attracts only boys I give a pep talk to get some girls to join. If children just can't figure out what group to join, I decide for them and move them into a group where I want more of a mix.

Rituals for Guided Research

Rituals add meaning and structure to our lives, giving a pattern to our days and helping children anticipate what will happen at school. Each class needs to develop rituals that fit its needs and situation. These are the rituals my class created to facilitate our 1998–99 research studies.

Stopping for a Hallway Greeting

I like the children to know what is happening before they enter the classroom, so every day when we reach the fourth floor, we stop in the hallway. I tell them if there are any trips, special events, or major changes in our schedule. I remind them if it is an interview day: "Today we will interview Julie's father, Anthony. What do you need to do to get ready for the interview?" I call on someone to tell the class to get their interview journals and a pencil. Because research groups may change from day to day, depending on what they are doing and which student teacher or family members are there, if it's a day for research groups, I tell the children where each group will meet:

- at a particular table
- on the carpet at story circle
- on mats in a particular area of the room

- at the door so they can go to the hallway or auditorium
- on the floor in the science area so they can work on their project

If our research is to be done by the whole class, I remind the children to get their research journals and go to the carpet at story circle.

Arriving in the Classroom

The ritual continues as we enter the classroom. The students hang up their coats, put their book bags away, put their homework folders in their mailboxes, and return the chairs to the tables. Many children glance at the schedule I have written on the board. A few children put the new date on our calendar or switch the day on our day chart. The children get their research journals from their cubbies and pencils from the pencil container, then go to bookshelves and cabinets to gather books, magazines, pictures, and other resources to take to their research groups.

After a few weeks, all of this is done without my help, and while the children are doing that I conduct business such as gathering notes about who's not going on the bus and who will be going where after school. I greet children and speak with the adults who make a quick stop in the room or who plan to stay and help. Of course, I have to remind the stragglers to get moving.

Conducting Research Workshop

Research Workshop can involve the whole class or separate research groups. At each Research Workshop, we try to find answers to our questions. The children use books, newspaper clippings, videos, music, and other resources and we have discussions and role-plays. We stop regularly so the children can record information in their research journals. Hands-on experiences include painting, doing experiments or observations, carving in soap, weaving, dancing, and other activities that enhance the children's understanding of the concepts.

Sharing the Research

After research groups have met for twenty to thirty minutes (sometimes longer), I say in a soft voice in Swahili, "Ah . . . go"—I want your attention. The children respond, "Ah . . . may"—we are listening. (These are phonetic spellings.) I tell the groups that they must stop in a few minutes. I sometimes hear, "Aw. Do we have to stop now?" I love to hear that, but I know that if we don't start Share Time right away, we could go on all day long.

Share Time is a crucial part of our research. Each group shares some of the highlights of their day's research. This should last ten to fifteen minutes, but we tend to go too long—there is so much enthusiasm, it's difficult to stop.

Moving On to the Rest of the Day

Inquiry is our curriculum, not an add-on to our curriculum, so what happens at Research Workshop or at an interview often extends into Reading Workshop, Math Workshop, Writing Workshop, or Center Time. It may even extend into the work at the specials such as science, art, music, and physical education. In our classroom, two days of Reading Workshop each week are dedicated to reading the homemade books from our interviews. Our research study is imbedded in the formal teaching of reading skills.

However, not everything must be part of a research study. During our Reading or Math Workshops, some activities may have no connection to our research study. Sometimes the read-alouds, songs, or poems at our class Meeting may be unrelated to the research study. It's not necessary to focus on the inquiry topic at every moment of the day. Some skills that we must teach just have no relationship to the inquiry topic, so trying to find a connection is unnecessary.

How Do We Begin a Research Study?

We begin every research study with three steps: tapping into prior knowledge, asking questions, and thinking of ways to search for answers to our questions.

Tapping into Prior Knowledge

What children already know about the topic will be the starting point of our research. In the process of children telling what they know, I often ask how they learned it. They may say they learned it from a parent, an uncle, a video, or a movie, or that they saw it somewhere. Some of the sources they name may be available to help us in the classroom.

Children who have prior knowledge of a topic can become teachers to their classmates, which can place a child with limited academic skills way ahead of his classmates or thrust a child whose participation has been limited into the limelight. This is wonderful for children's self-esteem. I have seen our research studies turn students around many, many times. Many children really blossom in an inquiry classroom.

When we tap into prior knowledge, we often uncover misinformation, stereotyping, or bias. Being aware of these can inform us of any "unlearning" we need to do.

Teachers must assume that children may know something about a given topic, even if it's just a little something. Sometimes just giving students a little information will remind them of something they already know. If all of the children are well informed about a topic, the research can begin at a more advanced level. If they have little prior knowledge, we must begin with the basics.

Tapping into prior knowledge

- validates what children already know
- empowers children to teach others, which makes them feel important and bolsters self-esteem.
- changes young children's perception that teachers and parents know everything
- may provide the group with a great deal of information
- may uncover misinformation that can be corrected in the research process
- may make the teacher aware of stereotyping and prejudice that must be addressed
- helps children get information in language that is appropriate for them
- gives adults a starting point for planning and continued research

Asking Questions

We always take time to ask questions. If children are in the early stages of writing, I write the questions on a chart or ask a parent or student teacher to write them down. If children are already writing fluently, they can write the questions. We save these lists so we can refer back to our questions. Like students' prior knowledge, these questions shape our planning.

Why do we ask questions?

- to find out the children's interests, which may be quite different from our own
- to determine the points of focus for our research
- to enable children to see that their questions are valued
- to teach children that asking questions is a strategy for learning
- to make our research studies multicultural to the greatest extent possible
- to reflect gender issues

Acquiring questioning skills is developmental. In the beginning of the year or in a class that has had no prior experience with research studies, there may be just a few questions or the questions may be limited in scope. If the children know little about a topic, we may have to help them formulate questions. As the year progresses, asking questions for new research topics gets easier: Later in the year, the questions will pour out.

Are the Teacher's Questions Acceptable? Of course, as long as they don't dominate the class's list. If I want to change the direction of the questions, I ask a question. Sometimes I add questions to broaden the scope of our inquiry or push critical thinking. Teachers can add questions to guarantee that the research study will deal with an issue they want to, or are required to, teach.

I often wait until the children have asked their questions to add mine. Sometimes I don't bring in my questions until the research is in progress.

How Can the Teacher Make the Research Study Include Issues of Diversity, Gender, or Economics? If I see the need to raise issues that will make our study multicultural, multiracial, multigendered, or about people whose economic backgrounds are different than families in our class, I ask or suggest the children ask questions that will raise those issues. For example, if the topic were houses, children might ask about big houses, small houses, and apartment buildings. I might say, "Is there someone who would like to ask about other kinds of houses, such as igloos, or houses made from mud, or shacks, or houses on water?" The children will start recalling different kinds of houses they have seen on TV, in pictures, or in their travels. Or I might ask, "Have any of you seen people who don't have any house and live on the street?" That will remind children of homeless people they have seen in person or on TV. They can't wait to include questions about homelessness. For the topic "Where do we get our food?" I might say, "I wonder if our fruits and vegetables are picked by adults or children? Is there someone here who would like to ask a question about that?"

Such questions are likely to lead to lively discussion, but the discussion should be kept brief, because we are asking questions, not answering them, at this point. The teacher is just whetting the students' appetite for research by broadening the scope of the questions.

If you pose such questions regularly, the children will see that you welcome all kinds of questions, including questions about serious issues or about people and things outside of their immediate experiences. The questions about big houses and small houses are great and should be encouraged, but we can also push children to look at things beyond their immediate consciousness, such as homelessness.

If you make a big deal out of a child's thought-provoking question, other children will ask thought-provoking questions. I might say, "Wow, that was an amazing question. I thought that only college kids asked those kinds of questions." This elevates the level of questions and expands the scope of the research study.

Did We Answer Our Questions? During and at the end of a research project, we return to our list of questions. I ask, "Did we answer this question yet?" We write "yes," "no," or "a little bit" or I make a red check to mean yes, a green check to mean we haven't answered the question yet.

If our research is still in progress, we may return to a question. If we are at the end of a formal research study and haven't gotten to a question, we acknowledge that. I may say, "Our vehicle research group won't be meeting any more. Does that mean you can never go back to this topic?" We laugh together as we acknowledge that research can go on forever.

Seeking Multiple Ways to Find Answers

The world is full of information, so much information that a teacher can be aware of only the tiniest fraction of it because a single person has relatively limited life experience.

In a traditional classroom there is a set of facts to be covered. A textbook represents a tiny fraction of information, often just a single point of view. Each text or curriculum guide reflects a point of view that is determined by the board of education, the school administration, or the teacher. It's fairly easy to give a test after that set of facts is imparted to the children. In an inquiry classroom there is not a finite set of facts, and there is not a single text or a single adult to teach that set of facts.

Guided research is developing strategies for finding information. Our goal is not so much to teach the facts or impart information, but to teach children ways to get information. What information and concepts we learn about depends on the resources we use. If we use a single source, we limit our learning. If we use multiple sources—interviews, books, trips, the Internet, and so on—we expand the learning. I introduce different kinds of resources little by little and work closely with students' families and my colleagues to expand the resources and perspectives the children can learn from.

What I love so much about guided research is that there are many detours and side stops on the way to the answers. Who would have guessed that we would find out that Dylan Levitt's great-grandfather helped repair elevators in coal mines, that Jordan Nassau comes from a family of coal miners, or that Ben Berkowitz's great-grandfather was a miner in the Netherlands? We learned all this on our route to finding out what vehicles are made from.

How Do We Plan a Research Study?

Once the topic or theme for a research study is determined, the planning begins. In 1998–99, I decided during the summer that our topic would be People at Work. I thought about what subtopics and issues I would like to raise. I wanted to be sure we would raise some new topics or issues and to return to some topics my previous classes had studied.

I thought about the families of my future class. I had already taught siblings from some of them, and I knew something about other families from talking with colleagues. This knowledge would inform my planning, but the starting point for planning is the questions of the children and their families. When we had those questions, my student teachers and I looked at them and decided which to start with and the most logical order for us to answer them in. Sometimes, to get the children hooked on the research, we started with the question that would provide a hands-on experience. Sometimes we started with the question for which we had the most resources. As we gathered other resources, we worked on other questions.

Seeing Guided Research as Interdisciplinary

The interdisciplinary nature of research studies is deliberate—it doesn't just happen. At every moment, I am looking for and thinking about ways to extend the research into every curriculum area. In the middle of an interview I might think to myself, "Oh, this would make a great topic for math." Or, "Wouldn't this make a fantastic science lesson?" There are several reasons to use an interdisciplinary approach:

- There are many ways for children to learn. Some love to read. Some love music. Others love hands-on art projects, or being in role-plays. Sometimes a trip will be a turning point for a child. Making our work interdisciplinary enables us to reach more children.
- Interdisciplinary work lets us focus on a topic and at the same time develop many skills.
- Interdisciplinary work helps children become critical thinkers whose thinking isn't compartmentalized—this is math, this is social studies, this is science. Children begin to see the relationships among disciplines.
- An interdisciplinary approach will enable children to make connections, see relationships, and think critically in the future.

Doing Interdisciplinary Planning. I have developed a planning chart to help my student teachers think in terms of interdisciplinary work. We often have brainstorming meetings where we use these charts (see Figure 2–1).

We can expand and enrich the possibilities for our studies if we work on the planning with students' families and our colleagues. Additional possibilities for activities will emerge as the research evolves. You won't be able to do everything you put on your chart. Some activities may not be age-appropriate, or you may not have enough time.

Planning to Raise Issues of Diversity and Gender

Once the children and adults have asked questions, we start planning how to turn concerns about gender and diversity into activities.

Getting Help with Our Planning

I consult with many people when I plan a research study. If you have never planned a research study, if you have had little experience with interdisciplinary planning, or if you need help thinking of ways to raise issues of diversity and gender, you can get help by

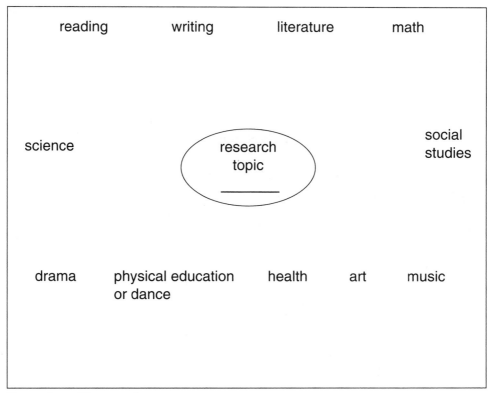

Figure 2–1. Planning chart.

- speaking with colleagues
- consulting with colleagues who teach special disciplines—music, art, science, physical education, or others. Perhaps they will even make your classroom research topics part of their own programs.
- speaking with students' family members
- consulting with educators outside of your school
- asking the children
- reading books on thematic teaching or inquiry teaching

Deciding How Long a Study Should Last

Research studies need time, lots of time. In *Going Public*, Shelley Harwayne (1999) says

> I want parents to understand why we value sticking with content studies for a long time . . . Schools become different places when people aren't rushing through curriculum, anxious to click off topics "covered." Instead, we value long-term commitment to fewer topics. (210)

A research study can begin with an approximate time frame, but because studies take twists and turns during the research, it is usually necessary to extend the time. We have also shortened the research when topics or subtopics didn't hold the children's interest.

Formal research about a particular topic might last a few weeks, a month, or the entire school year. The first year I decided to do a People at Work study with my first graders, I figured it would last about two months. When we were approaching two months, it felt like we were just beginning! That study continued for the rest of the school year.

What happens when you cannot decide how long to take for a study, when you have pacing calendars or other guidelines? If you cannot get special permission to extend the time or to do your own research study, consider doing parallel studies. I did this successfully in my previous school, where all work was controlled by pacing calendars and curriculum guides. The required topics took priority and I squeezed in research study topics whenever and however I could.

Parallel studies let you work on two unrelated topics at once. I want my class to do research about garbage and recycling every year, but the People at Work research study was the top priority for 1998–99. So, we had parallel studies, with People at Work as our main focus. We revisited the garbage and recycling research periodically, by digging up and observing the things we buried in our landfill; by interviewing Bobby De Cola, a sanitation worker who lives across from Manhattan New School; by watching a video about garbage; by making recycled paper; and more.

Thinking About How Much Time to Dedicate to a Research Study. We have Research Workshop four days a week, from twenty to forty-five minutes. One workshop is an interview with the whole class, either in the classroom or outside of school. Three times a week for Research Workshop is the minimum—once a week is not enough. Inquiry work takes place over time. If we don't give the children enough time to do that work and to return to it day after day, their experience is too limited. If there's too much time between Research Workshops there is a lack of continuity.

Finding Time for Research Studies

Teachers and students are already overloaded with work we must do. How can we find time for yet another thing to do? Making the research study interdisciplinary and using time well are the main solutions.

Assessing Our Management Practices. If we want to have time for research, we must ask questions about our management practices and schedules. What can we do to find time for Research Workshop and interviews? Here are some things to think about:

- What are your expectations? Do the children know your expectations for them?
- How long does it take to get the children's attention?
- How long are your transitions from reading to math, or from research to reading?
- How long does it take to get into line for lunch?
- Can these activities be done more efficiently?
- What can you do to help the children understand their role during transitions?
- Does your body language match your words?

My students quickly realize that I am serious about our work and that I love to have fun as we learn. They learn that the more respectful they are to each other and to the adults in the classroom, the more we get to do, the more we learn, and the more fun we have. I don't tolerate antisocial behavior. The whole class works together to turn such behavior around because it is unacceptable and we just don't have time for that "nonsense."

I keep my voice low all day, and after a while, the children do too. That makes the classroom calm, and the calm enables children to speak and to be heard. I spend relatively little time quieting everyone down, which gives us more time for research. If I must reprimand a child, I lower my voice rather than shout.

Even after twenty-five years of teaching, I'm still looking for strategies for maximizing teaching time. Last year I assigned new line partners each month because I saw that too much time and energy were being wasted while children selected their own partners. Some years I assign spots on the carpet to reduce the amount of time needed for getting settled.

Positive reinforcement works to speed things along. Children love to be complimented. We compliment (not thank) children who help with quick cleanups during transitions, get in line quickly, and help each other. Other children then begin to do these things because they want a compliment, too.

We have a few signals for silence. These signals are absolutes, not maybes. There are consequences if the rules and the signals are not respected.

All of these efforts result in real time for inquiry studies.

Thinking and Rethinking Your Schedule. If research studies are a priority, something else must go to make time for Research Workshop. Examine your schedule.

I looked at my traditional morning meeting, where I used to go over the date, the day, the weather, the schedule, and news or show-and-tell. The meeting took twenty to thirty minutes, so I decided to eliminate it. Instead, I created an afternoon Meeting filled with poetry, song, and literature. This new format and meeting time enriched our research studies. I found other ways to deal with the things we used to do in morning meeting:

- The date. Right away in September, I show the children where I write the date near the schedule and how to read the calendar, so they can date their journals and other work.
- The weather. If there is something special about the weather, the children will be sure to let me know! There have been many times over the years when a student noticed it was snowing and pandemonium broke out.
- The news. Important news can be woven into the day.
- Show and tell. We eliminated the traditional show and tell. When children brought things that were related to our research, they showed it to the class during Research Workshop or Share Time.

Our daily schedule in 1998–99 looked like this:

Research Workshop and Share Time
Reading Workshop
Science (once a week or woven into the day, since the children have two special science classes outside the classroom)
Math Workshop
Writing Workshop
Lunch
Special Subjects taught by other teachers (music, art, science, science research, physical education)
Meeting (poetry, singing, and a story)
Center Time

The schedule varied because the special subjects were not always at the same time. Each period was approximately twenty to forty-five minutes. We had to be flexible. Center Time was from fifteen to thirty minutes. The children were content as long as they had *some* Center Time.

Sometimes Writing Workshop wasn't long enough. The children loved to write, but we had to go to lunch. On those days, we agreed to leave our writing where it was and come back to it in the afternoon. Is that sound educational practice? Maybe not, but it was the best we could do given the limited number of hours in the day. The children adjusted to it very well because of their passion for writing.

Some days I worried because there wasn't enough time for one of the curriculum areas that day. I comforted myself by remembering that Research Workshop often involved reading, writing, literature, math, and science.

What Happens During Research Workshop?

There's no one right way to run Research Workshops—they can look so different from one teacher to another or from one day to the next.

Doing Different Types of Activities

Young children seem to learn best when they are doing, making, feeling, or seeing. You will want to look in fiction and nonfiction books, read newspaper or magazine articles, and watch videos, but it's important to have more active learning, too, so the Research Workshop must include experiential learning. Here are some ways to make learning active:

- If you are reading a book or an article, stop to do role-plays, then have a brief discussion. This helps build a deeper understanding of the concepts you read about, and it's fun—it keeps the interest level high.
- After you have developed an understanding of a topic, write a skit about it. Practice the skit, then present it to the class or to the students' families.
- Do art work to deepen understanding about a concept. The children might work with clay or plasticine, paint, linoleum, crayons, colored pencils or markers, or wood. Projects might include paintings, collages, murals, dioramas, posters, and quilts.
- Replicate what you are reading about. One time during a research study about the work of paleontologists, we preserved some chicken bones by wrapping them with burlap coated with plaster, just as a real expedition to Madagascar we read about had done to preserve bones for future study. It was messy and fun, and I'm sure the children will remember it for years.
- Build with blocks to help illustrate—and help the children experience—a concept. Once the children built a coal mine in the block area. Another time they built several buildings from blocks and used paper towel rolls and fabric rolls to represent water and gas pipes and electric and phone lines. This work continued for weeks.
- Listen to music, sing, or write songs related to the inquiry topic.
- Read, recite, or write poetry related to the inquiry topic.
- Write small or big books about the topic. Each child can contribute pages that can be stapled together or glued into a book.
- Produce videos about the topic and show them to an audience. You can create real videos or paper mock-ups, putting the sound on a cassette tape.
- Dance or create dances related to the topic.
- Go on related trips.

Constructing Answers to Our Questions

We need to create dialogue around hands-on activities, many of which stimulate discussion. Participating in a multitude of activities and discussions over time lets the children construct meaning and find answers to their questions. Talk happens after a role-play or when children are making a model with clay or painting and their thoughts, feelings, and more questions arise. Sometimes the discussion is teacher-directed. Other times we overhear the children's conversations and take notes so we can pursue their comments another time.

Becoming a Facilitator of Inquiry

As children respond to activities, we adults listen. How should we respond? Do we wait for the children to respond to each other? Do we let them move away from the questions of the day, or do we keep them focused? We must use our judgment about responding, and that takes practice. It's tempting to jump in and answer questions, but sometimes we must hold back and let the children do the work.

Even if you are used to telling children the answers, you can transform your classroom and become a facilitator of inquiry. Here's how:

- Ask questions, questions, and more questions.
- Let children and their families ask questions, questions, and more questions.
- Stop yourself from giving the answers.
- Turn the children's questions back to them. "What do you think about this?" "Does anyone have a way we can solve this problem?" "Why do you think that?" "Could there be another answer?"
- Help the children think of different ways to answer the questions.
- Use multiple resources so it's not just the teacher providing all the answers.
- Give the children time to search for answers, exchange ideas, and formulate answers.
- Seek out different ideas and different ways of formulating thoughts.
- Encourage full participation by all children. Some children listen and participate actively, while others need help learning to listen and participate. As you search for answers, you need everyone's thinking. Shy, inactive, or disabled children have important thoughts—it's important to think about ways to get them involved in the discussions.

Dealing with Complex or Difficult Issues

Sometimes we tackle difficult issues. First graders and other young children are very perceptive. They can understand complex issues if we take several steps:

- Simplify the issue. What essential concepts do you want the children to understand? Are there certain concepts or facts about which you would like the children to get a lasting impression? Focus on these things.
- Role-play so children can visualize the information or the concept. The children in my class began to understand the concept of a sweatshop from role-play, not from a theoretical discussion. Young children are quite literal. They develop an understanding of a concept from seeing it or visualizing it. Think about which facts or concepts you want the children to remember and plan role-plays accordingly. Allow time for questions and discussion after the role-play and ask questions to see if the children understand. If they don't, do the role-play again. See what you can change to make the concept more clear.
- Ask children or family members to translate for children who are just learning English. If no one speaks the child's language, challenge the class to figure out a way to explain things to the child.
- Go back to the same topic day after day, using different examples or activities. It often takes repeated work on an issue to develop understanding.
- When visitors or children from other classes are in your room, have the children explain what they are learning. That lets them review the information and develop a deeper understanding. Perhaps the visitors will add new information.
- Tell the families what you did and provide related activities in the Family Homework. This gives the children an opportunity to discuss the issues again and to hear other viewpoints, and lets them practice using the information or concepts.

Combating Misinformation, Stereotyping, and Prejudice

Early in the school year, I talk with the student teachers about combating misinformation, stereotyping, and prejudice.

You can respond immediately to prejudice or stereotyping, but you don't have to. Sometimes it's better to step back and take some time to think about how you will deal with it. Maybe a coworker or family member will have some suggestions. A well thought-out response later is better than a mediocre immediate response. You can go to the children after a time and say, "I was thinking about what someone said the other day when Pam was reading the Chinese story. I want us to take some time now to think about that."

Responding to prejudice and stereotyping is a year-long effort in our classroom. We talk about prejudice or stereotyping as it relates to a specific incident, but I also raise these issues throughout the year. Extending the study over time rather than simply saying "that's wrong" or "that's a stereotype" helps the children develop a deeper understanding.

Role-plays help create understanding. I usually have children play different roles, taking turns being the object of discrimination or the person who's acting in a prejudiced way.

Coming to terms with stereotyping involves researching the facts. What information is correct information? Are there different ways of looking at the same thing? How do we find accurate information?

Have the discussion in front of the families, too, at a meeting or in the Family Homework. Sometimes this stimulates great discussions at home, reinforcing your effort to eliminate prejudice. Sometimes it brings out a family's prejudice and gives children a chance to discuss this with their own family members.

Becoming More Conscious of Resources

For young children, it's important to know that we get information from all over the place—from people, books, TV, movies, experience, ads, computers, and more.

It's also important for children to be able to check the validity of a source. When my student teacher noticed lots of stereotyping about Chinese and Asian people, we had a class discussion. The children made a long list of what they knew about Chinese people, some of it accurate, some of it stereotypes. Rather than attack the children by challenging the stereotypes, I first asked, "Where did you get that information?" They said they'd gotten it from movies and TV, from their friends, and from their parents. Why did I ask? It's important for children to begin to realize that not all information is correct and some sources have to be evaluated or challenged. Our class challenged some of the stereotypes and even wondered why our sources gave us that information. This challenging can begin in early childhood classrooms and intensify as children get older.

I make a big deal about sources to encourage children to return to their sources in the future and assess them. There are a number of ways to develop children's awareness about sources:

- Ask, "Where did you get that information?" or "How did you learn about that?" Your tone should be friendly, not challenging.
- Praise a child who finds a new source of information. Make a big deal about it. "Ashley and Paulina found information about Woody Guthrie on this stamp. That's amazing. You mean, you can learn about a person by looking at postage stamps? That's great." Praise sets off a chain reaction—other children will come up with sources we never thought of.

- Don't limit your request for sources of information to Research Workshop—ask at any point in the day. Keep the families informed about your interest and your reasons for wanting to develop multiple ways of gathering information. I do this in the Family Homework, at Curriculum Night, and in individual discussions. My hope is that families will use this research model at home, making it a way of life.

Developing a Community of Learners

There's a natural tension built into the process of doing guided research because we are constructing knowledge together and because there is no script. As children seek answers, new questions arise and controversial issues emerge. Sometimes there's a consensus; sometimes there are disagreements. Teachers have the difficult job of helping children learn together and work cooperatively. That's not always easy, even in a relatively small research group. In the excitement of an activity or discussion, some children tend to dominate and others are pushed into the background. We want lively discussions, but we strive to involve all members of the group.

Our class has rules to ensure that everyone can participate. We don't post a list of the rules, but introduce them as we work and review them as needed.

Rules for children:
- Raise your hand and wait to be called on. (I wish we didn't need this, but it allows for greater participation by all children.)
- Put your hand down when another person is speaking.
- Look at the person who is talking or focus on the thing they are talking about.
- Do not laugh at people's ideas unless they were meant to be funny.
- Don't call others names if you don't agree or don't like the way something was said.
- Keep your voices low if there are other people working in different parts of the room.
- Keep pencils down during a discussion unless an adult wants you to record information. This eliminates doodling, tapping, and poking.

Rules for adults:
- Constantly look to see who is or is not participating in an activity or discussion.
- Encourage or help children who are not participating. It's often best to think about this before Research Workshop because it's usually the same children. Here are some ways to help:

> Speak to the child before Research Workshop to encourage him to participate.
> Have a parent or volunteer work with the child in the group.
> Assign a partner to work with the child.
> Have the child sit next to the teacher.
> Call on the child even if his hand is not raised.
> Tell the child that you will be calling on her in a few moments.
> Remind the other children to wait for the child to formulate his thoughts.
> Compliment children: "Great idea." "Good Thinking."
> Give special compliments to children who have made a breakthrough in their participation.

You can really feel that you have a community of learners when children praise each others' work, ideas, and participation; when someone walks into the room and the children are bouncing with enthusiasm to talk about what they're learning; or when the children present songs, poems, a play, a dance, a mural, or a project at a Family Celebration. A community of learners feels like a "we," not an "I." That feeling can last forever in our memories.

Why Do We Share Our Research?

There's a little-known verse in Woody Guthrie's song "This Land Is Your Land":

> As I went walking, I saw a sign there
> On the sign it said "No Trespassing"
> But on the other side it didn't say nothing
> That side was made for you and me.

Our research is public and it's meant to be shared. We don't have private property in our class, other than our clothing, journals, and book bags. Our research groups have lots of experiences, not all of which we have time to share with the whole class. But we work to find ways to bring as much information as possible about a research topic to the whole class and beyond. Sharing knowledge means empowering children to teach other people, including other children and adults.

Sharing is important to our inquiry classroom in many ways:

- The class continues to construct knowledge or concepts as they share, listen, make connections, add ideas, and add information during Share Time.
- Sharing not only gives the children a chance to review their work, it also enables them to become teachers and to see each other as teachers.
- Sharing lets teachers and children sort information and decide what is most important or relevant to communicate to others.
- Children learn how to communicate more effectively.

- Children learn to listen to each other.
- Sharing is a form of social action.

Creating Rituals to Facilitate Sharing

Our class shares in many ways:

- We share our research with nearly every adult who enters our room: teachers, the principal, family members, and visitors. This lets the children review the information and concepts. Adults often bring new information and insights, giving the children another opportunity to construct knowledge.
- We form cooperative research groups where children and adults share materials, ideas, and information through discussion and activities.
- When we work in different research groups, we have Share Time at the end of Research Workshop.
- At Meeting after a read-aloud, we have book talk, where we share our thinking.
- At Meeting and even at dismissal time we share songs the children may have learned during Research Workshop.
- At Center Time the children often use the block area or dress-up area for research-related activities. For example, during the research study about health care workers, the block area became a hospital and the children used the dress-up clothes for the hospital. Children from different groups may work together in the block or dress-up area, making the Research Workshop experience a shared one.
- Research topics are the core of the Family Homework. Every week we share information about the work of each research group with the families.
- We paint some of the research-related murals at Center Time so that everyone can participate. As many children as possible make labels or signs for the murals so they feel like part of the mural projects. We post the murals in the room and in the surrounding halls so that the whole class will see them and can refer to them regularly. We share the murals with our whole school and with visitors so that they will learn about our topics.
- Children share their thoughts by making comments at the end of each interview.
- Children share their thinking about interviews and trips when they write pages for homemade books. We share our homemade books with the families and people outside our class.
- We encourage all the students to write about each others' research topics during Writing Workshop and to share their writing at the end of Writing Workshop or at Meeting.

- We talk about links between different research topics, or between research topics and literature. When I read *Nobody Owns the Sky: The Story of "Brave Bessie" Coleman*, about the first black woman pilot in the United States, someone commented that she was brave like Elizabeth Blackwell, the first woman doctor in the United States. That topic was from the health workers research.
- We search for resources from all the families, not just the research group's families. Our research is a shared effort.
- We write and present plays to our class, then share them with class families and our school.
- We make pictures, photographs, murals, books, and videos that we share.

How Can We Move from Inquiry to Social Action?

Social action means becoming an agent for change. To be most effective, you need to be informed. My students become informed through guided research or inquiry.

In her anti-bias curriculum, Louise Derman-Sparks (1989) encourages teachers to help children create social change beyond the classroom in ways that are relevant to their understanding of bias and fairness. Like Derman-Sparks, I believe that social change starts within the classroom, then goes beyond it, or starts within the home, then goes beyond it. Ideally, we want the school and the families to work together for social change, and we want families' social consciousness to be welcome in our classroom.

Social action ranges from simply sharing your learning with others to marching on picket lines or attending rallies. There's so much in between. My goal is to make children conscious of the need for social action and enable them to see social action as a way of life. My classes have used many forms of social action, both in the classroom and at after-school events where the children's adult family members joined us. We have

- discussed issues with classmates, families, and other people outside of school
- written letters expressing an opinion
- written and self-published books and distributed poems about social issues
- written and performed plays about social issues
- made phone calls to express an opinion or urge a specific outcome
- participated in events at individual schools or school districts, or in city- or countywide efforts. Events included meetings, writing contests, art exhibitions, concerts, and drama programs. In the district I taught in before, I worked with a group of teachers to persuade the school board to have a yearly districtwide celebration of Black History Month. Each of the district schools presented a song, play, dance, or orchestra performance. The yearly celebration has happened for nearly twenty years.

- participated in efforts by organizations including trade unions and community groups. Efforts included meetings, writing contests, art exhibitions, concerts, and drama programs.
- made or signed petitions
- participated in boycotts
- spoken at or attended government hearings
- marched in or attended vigils and rallies
- raised money for fire or storm victims, and for schools and clinics in areas of need
- collected food and clothing for soup kitches and homeless shelters

In March 1999, our child labor research group did a role-play about children working in a factory that made artificial flowers. When it was Share Time, I wouldn't let the group join the class. I made them stay at their table with the student teacher and pretend to keep working. They continued their role-play in front of the whole class. A few children pretended to be injured by sharp cutting tools. Some pretended to have sore hands from doing the same job over and over. Some complained about low pay and long hours. The children got to experience for a few minutes what it was like to not be able to go to school.

That role-play inspired Phoebe to write about the child laborers during Writing Workshop. At Meeting that afternoon, Phoebe shared her poem with the class, reading with such passion and full expression that I practically lost my breath. When I recovered, I said, "Phoebe, your poem is fantastic, it must become a mural." At Center Time we began work on the mural. (See Figure 2–2.)

While arranging a field trip, I mentioned Phoebe's poem and our mural to Esther Cohen of Bread and Roses, a cultural project of Local 1199 of the Health and Hospital Workers Union. She was preparing an exhibition of student art about sweatshops and child labor, a joint project of Bread and Roses, the Union of Needletrades Industrial and Textile Employee's (UNITE) Stop Sweatshops campaign, the New York City Department of Cultural Affairs, and the New York State Labor-Religion Coalition. Esther grabbed up the poem and mural to exhibit at Local 1199 and then become part of a national traveling exhibit. When our class was invited to attend the opening of the exhibition on the evening of May 20, many families attended. Phoebe recited her poem to a packed hall.

I included Phoebe's poem in the Family Homework, not just because it was so great, but because I knew it would inspire passionate writing by other children. And it did.

In May 1999, our class produced a play, *The Person Behind the Thing,* that enabled us to move from research studies to social action, spreading the word about

Figure 2–2. A class mural about Phoebe's poem, *Child Labor*.

child labor and sweatshops. It posed options for bringing about change. In fact, one of the lines in the songs is,

> I can change the world
> 'Cause I can help make people see.

Doing the play helped the children move from feeling so sad and helpless about the terrible problem of child labor and sweatshops to feeling that they were helping to make things better.

Each new person who is made aware of a social problem can become an agent of change. If we teach children ways to take action and to become part of the solution, we give them hope for the future. A school play of this nature stays in your heart and mind forever. The content of this play was really significant. So, perhaps the children's concern about child labor and sweatshops will continue for years to come.

Nancy Schniedewind and Ellen Davidson discuss the concept of children becoming social activists in their sourcebook *Cooperative Learning, Cooperative Lives* (1987). Barbara Lewis wrote an entire book on this topic, *The Kid's Guide to Social Action* (1991). Both books are jam-packed with suggestions.

Finding Resources

In *The BIG Picture: Integrating Children's Learning* (1993), Keith Pigdon and Marilyn Woolley write

The way we use resources often determines their effectiveness in sustaining students' learning. Resources should allow students to make connections with their own prior knowledge and experiences, but they also need to take them beyond their current knowledge base . . . The key question is: Are they rich enough to develop understandings? (86)

The teacher can't and doesn't have to know a lot about every topic the children propose for a research study. Then what can we do to provide resources? The teacher must be a researcher, working behind the scenes in school and at home to make sure the children have a variety of traditional and nontraditional resources. Having a variety of resources gives children a chance to learn about multiple perspectives, provides a greater range of information, and enables both children and teacher to get a deeper understanding.

For example, if children are learning about immigration, a textbook will have some information, but may offer only one perspective. People immigrate for many reasons, and there are many opinions about immigration. People arrive in other countries in different ways and under different conditions. By using other resources—conducting interviews, reading autobiographies, seeing videos, and going to arrival locations such as Ellis Island—the children have a chance to develop broad and deep understanding of immigration.

Including Multicultural Resources

Using resources that represent diversity opens up new worlds and new issues to our students and ourselves. I want the curriculum to reflect both the children themselves and people who are different from them. We must accumulate a range of resources (both human and material) that are multicultural—that reflect diversity in their content. Resources must also reflect a diverse range of people—book authors, video producers, and interview subjects. I think about the need for diversity as I plan for interviews.

One year the children wanted to do research about book illustrators. I wanted my student teacher, Debbie Ardemendo, to present a few possibilities to her research group to guarantee that the children would study illustrators of different backgrounds. She and I looked through the picture books in our classroom and thought about which illustrators would be best for the research study. Then we gathered the books of five diverse illustrators: illustrators who were older and younger; men and women; black, white, Asian, and Hispanic. The children looked through the books and chose two illustrators for their research.

The children spent two months doing research about Vera B. Williams, an older, white, female author and illustrator, and Brian Pinkney, a young, male, African American illustrator. The research group shared daily with the whole class, who fell in love with the two illustrators. We ended up reading their books at Meeting. At Center Time, children painted a mural of a page from Williams' book *A Chair for My Mother* and did scratch-art on the type of scratch-art paper Brian Pinkney uses.

Debbie worked hard to arrange interviews with both illustrators. Our class took a school bus to Williams' studio, and Williams came to our Family Celebration, where we introduced her to the families and honored her for enriching our lives. We interviewed Pinkney in our classroom. Both are spectacular illustrators and are extraordinary human beings and role models.

Adapting Resources

Most curricula for early childhood require us to teach about a select group of "community helpers": police, fire, and postal workers. There are lots of books and other resources about those workers. But if we reach beyond those jobs to the vast range of jobs held by students' families or others in our school community, most teachers will be at a loss for resources. One of the big problems we face in inquiry classrooms is the limited number of resources that are age-appropriate. We often find ourselves working to adapt resources, doing even more outreach and making creative use of resources that may not be age-appropriate.

Before I use books, videos, or other resources, I preview them. Students may end up looking at just a small section of a book or watching only a few segments of a video. When we wanted to know more about how the steel used in vehicles is made, most of the books we found were for older children and adults. We used them anyway, using several ways to make them appropriate: At Research Workshop we looked in books' indexes. We looked at pictures and captions. Adults paraphrased or summarized information from the books. Often the children role-played the content to help them understand the information.

Finding New Ways to Use Old Resources

After the children choose a new topic, I comb through the classroom looking for poems and fiction and nonfiction books. Perhaps some of them can be used in new ways. When children were doing research about the Caribbean Islands, they wanted to know about the trees and flowers, the fruits and vegetables, and the clothing. I suggested that they look at Monica Gunning's poems in *Not a Copper Penny in Me House* (1993). We had recited many of those poems over and over at Meeting. This time, the children looked not only at the poems, but at the beautiful illustrations by Frané Lessac. They were excited to find that this book we loved so much was useful in a new way.

If you take a second look at children's picture books that are considered classics, you will find social studies, science, and even math concepts. These books have the potential to be used multiple ways. Perhaps their richness of content is what makes them last for generations.

The African folktale *Mufaro's Beautiful Daughters*, retold by John Steptoe (1987), is a delightful story for read-alouds, but you can also use it in other ways. It offers a fine example of the contrast between good and bad, and it's of one of the few stories available in the United States where the king is not only handsome and good, but black. You can use the words and illustrations to learn about traditions and about crops and other plants in Africa. To learn more about peddlers, we reread the classic *Caps for Sale*, by Esphyr Slovbodkina (1968). To learn about construction, basements, and foundations, we reread *Mike Mulligan and His Steam Shovel*, by Virginia Lee Burton (1939).

Seeing the World as a Resource

Seeing through the lens of the classroom is quite different from seeing though the lens of the world, so we make the world our classroom We start the year with neighborhood walking trips, working on appropriate trip behavior. We expand to school bus and subway trips (with a large group of adults to assist us). Soon our class has access to the entire city and beyond.

Our research often takes us into the community. During trips we do observations, take notes, and have on-the-spot discussions or interviews. Afterwards we take time to process and write about what we have seen.

Sometimes the children ask people they meet for their autographs, as if they are movie stars, athletes, or superheroes. They *are* heroes. They are the workers who build our city and provide the many services, who create music and art and dance. There are so many role models for the children.

Over the years my classes have gone on trips to

- family members' job sites, including the buildings of parents who are superintendents, the subway where a parent drove the train, hospitals, restaurants, art studios, and recording studios
- students' apartments and my house
- factories
- museums and galleries
- ferry boats in the harbor
- Indian caves
- union halls
- the schools of our pen pals in New York and in other cities and states
- a school that created a museum about life in Harlem long ago
- zoos
- parks

- farms
- art studios
- a bus depot
- stores and restaurants
- environmental centers
- a parade to welcome former South African president Nelson Mandela (as part of a study on apartheid and South Africa)
- the 92nd Street Y
- the middle of the Brooklyn Bridge, where we interviewed the workers
- the middle of the George Washington Bridge, where we met a peace delegation that had marched across the United States

Interviewing People

Can you remember the time your parent or other relative came to your elementary school for an interview? Can you remember a teacher who thought of your family members as primary sources of information? Can you imagine using a book about your parent as the reading lesson?

In our inquiry-based classroom, students' families and the people in the community are a primary source of information. What they bring to the children is far beyond the reach of any textbook: They bring facts, details, thoughts, feelings, insights, laughter, sadness, and concerns.

Interviews are personal. The children often bond with the person we interview, who becomes like a family member or friend and who seems to care about us.

Interviews are a wonderful resource for young children. We can adjust an interview to meet the students' needs and learning styles. During an interview the teacher is constantly accessing the children's level of understanding and taking steps to raise it:

- If the person being interviewed says something that is over the children's heads, we can stop the interview to have a discussion or do a role-play to make sure the children understand.
- If the person talks too quickly, has a heavy accent, or speaks in another language, we can stop and interpret for the children.
- If the person tells the children too many details, we can decide what, of all the things the person is saying, is most important for the children to know, then communicate those things to the children in a discussion or role-play.
- If many children don't seem to understand what the person is saying, we can stop to have the person repeat what they have said, have a discussion, or do a role-play.

What Resources Did We Use During 1998–99?

In September, when I asked the children where we could find information to answer our questions, they suggested three resources: books, the teacher, and our parents. That grew to a very long list by the end of the year, a list that many of the children, their families, the student teachers, and I will draw on for the rest of our lives when we seek answers to our questions.

- Think in our brain.
- Ask questions of anyone—family, neighbors, babysitters, friends, workers, and so on.
- Interview people.
- Take trips to factories, museums, galleries, houses, parks, and other towns, cities, or countries
- Use these resources:
  - nonfiction books
  - fiction books (stories and folktales)
  - poetry
  - the Internet
  - magazines
  - newspapers
  - plays, skits, the theater
  - music—live performances, CDs, tapes, records
  - jackets or covers of CDs, tapes, records
  - stamps
  - clothing, traditional and modern
  - uniforms
  - art—drawings, paintings, photographs, murals, lithographs
  - signs
  - posters
  - TV shows
  - videos
  - movies
  - maps and atlases
  - dictionaries
  - food
  - dances
  - buildings, streets, rivers or other bodies of water, bridges
  - languages
  - children's games
  - toys

- plants, gardens, forests, deserts, parks
- animals and their habitats
- experiments

Getting Help Finding Resources

Finding resources is tough, especially for new teachers who haven't yet accumulated them. It's also difficult when children choose a topic that is totally new to the teacher. If you have absolutely no resources and no prospects for finding them, shift the children to a new topic.

Remember that when we are talking about resources, we're not just talking about books. The families always help. When twenty-six families are looking, instead of just me, we find many resources. I reach out to families through the Family Homework, special notes, and individual discussions in person or on the phone, and I ask the children to inquire at home. (In the Appendix, see the Family Homework from September 15.)

We get resources from my colleagues and from other classes at school. Our principal and colleagues can direct us to classrooms that may have appropriate resources. Sometimes teachers or students post signs requesting help with resources. Our classroom research also extends into my home life. By talking with friends and family members, I not only get suggestions for how to proceed with a research study—I often get more resources.

Where Else Can We Look for Resources? There are a number of other sources:

- garage sales and flea markets
- used-book stores
- used-book sales at libraries
- book fairs
- freebies:
    - check for notices of free materials in the union newspaper or local newspapers
    - ask stores, museums, and travel agencies for free materials

Paying for Resources

If your school has a limited budget, you can

- contact publishers
- apply for grants
- ask the Parent-Teacher Association for funds
- raise money at bake sales or other fund-raisers.

The PTA at Manhattan New School has two book fairs a year. At both fairs there is a box in which teachers can put books we would like for our classrooms. A family can buy one of the books and donate it to the classroom, and we'll put their name inside the front cover. The PTA also holds a street fair at which teachers and families can buy used books and materials.

Assessing Children as They Do Research

Assessment is critical and every child is important. When we do our planning, we must take into account children's different learning styles and abilities. Ongoing assessment informs our planning and our teaching. We assess children informally by

- observing and listening to discussions at Research Workshop
- observing at role-plays and subsequent discussions
- observing and listening to discussions during Meeting, Writing Workshop, Math Workshop, and even Center Time, when the discussion is related to the research
- looking at children's writing to assess spelling, grammar, punctuation, the ability to express themselves, and the children's understanding of the issues

We ask ourselves questions:

- How much is a child participating in the discussions? If there is very little or no participation, why? How can the adults work to increase participation?
- Is the child's input relevant to the discussion at hand?
- Does the child seek to relate things to her own life?
- Does the child listen to the other children and adults?
- How analytical is the child?
- Is the child a critical thinker?
- Does the child see connections and relationships?
- How enthusiastic is the child about the research? If he has little enthusiasm, why? Is it lack of interest, lack of sleep, an inability to concentrate, or poor planning by the adults?

One year I had the children complete a form called "Thinking of Myself as a Researcher." It was useful near the end of first grade when the children really did think of themselves as researchers and had the writing skills to express their thoughts.

Summary

You can always tell when children have been in an inquiry classroom. They're good at formulating questions and digging for answers. They've had experience working in groups. They know the thrill of finding links between issues and the joy of working with others to ask, seek, and find answers. My greatest hope is that questioning and digging will become a lifestyle for my students, and that they will use their knowledge to help make this a better world.

3

Family Involvement

Family Involvement Is Fundamental

The children and their families are the heart and soul of our research. (I usually refer to "families" rather than "parents" because a number of my students have lived with grandparents, aunts and uncles, or guardians.) Family involvement empowers families to become even more involved in their children's education, both at home and at school. This empowerment is critical in an inquiry classroom.

Families are among the greatest resources a teacher will encounter, and no matter where you teach, families are guaranteed resources of human experience. With a class of twenty-five children, you have potential access to fifty or a hundred people—the childrens' immediate families, their extended families, and the families' friends, contacts, and coworkers. Imagine the power of all those people working together for the children.

I say "potential" access because family participation involves a lot of effort and time on the part of teachers and other school personnel. I use myriad ways to tap into this most valuable resource—the families.

Teaching the Whole Child

Over the years I've heard some teachers say, "I don't care what's going on at home. This child has to pay attention to me." But a child is not simply the person who sits in our classroom. A child is a whole human being who reflects their prenatal circumstances, living conditions, experiences in and outside of the home, cultural or spiritual life, and other societal influences. A child has interests, needs, talents, hobbies, and concerns, and so do the members of a child's family.

Knowing the whole child helps me be a better teacher. If I know that a child loves to dance or play soccer, it helps me select books for the child to read or a topic for the child to write about in Writing Workshop.

Certain issues come up whether you're working in a middle-income or poor neighborhood. A child's family members may be preoccupied with work or hobbies, or work during the evening or night so they're not accessible to the child. A family may have serious economic problems, or be experiencing separation or divorce. A child or a family member may have health or mental health problems, or problems with substance or alcohol abuse. There may be fighting or abuse in the child's home, or a family member may be in jail.

When teachers establish a close working relationship with a family, little by little we get to know the whole child. Families' observations and insights about children inform our teaching and help us better understand children's behavior. I have found that many children who visit their fathers or mothers on weekends are often still processing the experience on Monday morning. Knowing that helps me be more understanding, rather than puzzled by a child's lack of focus. I talk privately with that child and work hard to draw him into our activities. It also helps me to know if a child is out-of-sorts because her parents are going through a divorce.

Relatives know that they can talk with me about family matters because I make it clear that I am accessible to them. If a parent or other relative wants, I can talk privately with a child to remind him that I know what's happening at home and to sympathize. I can allow him to write about his situation at Writing Workshop, or help him get refocused on the work. Just knowing that the teacher knows about the home situation can be such a relief that it enables a child to function at a higher level.

Knowing that a child is deprived of love or a feeling of safety within the family drives me to search for ways to make our classroom as loving and as safe as possible. Knowing that a family cannot afford class trips or books at the book fair informs how I raise money to ensure that everyone can participate. Knowing that a child has not been read to at home inspires me even more to fill the year with literature and to try to get the family to read to the child.

One year when I taught in Washington Heights, I read Else Minirek's *Little Bear* books with my students. Most of the children spoke Spanish at home. Once they could read them fairly fluently, they took the books home, along with a note from me written in Spanish and English. I asked the children whose parents spoke little or no English to teach their parents to read their book. We had a Little Bear party with bear cakes and other goodies. Leaning against pillows as parents took turns reading the story. For some parents, it was a struggle and a triumph. When I look at the video of that marvelous event, I smile because we accomplished several things:

- We brought literature into homes that had never seen it before.
- We empowered the children to teach their families.
- We helped some families develop the ritual of reading at home.
- We made learning a joy.
- We encouraged more adults to participate in their children's education at home and in school.
- We deepened the bond between home and school.
- We deepened the bond between adults and their children.
- We acknowledged the whole child.

Building Good Working Relationships

If we truly want families to get involved with their children's education, we must show them so with our own behavior. We don't have to be friends with the families, although I often choose to be, but we do need to make every effort to develop good working relationships.

Have a Positive Attitude Toward Families

Our success in involving family members depends mostly on our attitude toward the families. If we have a positive attitude, families will know it and respond in kind. Through meetings, informal conversations, and the Family Homework, we tell families

- You are intelligent people, whether you are college-educated or have completed only elementary school.
- You have a variety of life experiences from which we can learn.
- We can learn about different races, cultures, and nationalities from you.
- Whether you are rich, poor, or in-between, you are equal in our eyes.
- We can learn from your big range of work experiences.
- You can introduce us to lots of other people from your family, your work, and your neighborhood.
- You may be shy or afraid to speak to our whole class, but we'll help you with that.
- You may not know how to reach out to young children other than your own, but we'll help with that. Don't hesitate to come into our classroom.
- You may be too busy to be involved, with babies at home or a full time job, but we'll help with that.
- You love your child, but may not know how to work with her or reach out to him. We'll work together on that.

- There is a teacher who is in the classroom all day, but, you, the family members, are teachers, too.

Take the Initiative

Here are things that I try to do to develop my working relationships with families. As you look at this list, assess your own attitude toward working with families.

- Greet family members in a friendly way.
- Take time to talk informally.
- Tell family members that I want their participation.
- Reach out to family members who are not participating because of language differences, fear, or shyness; because they're not part of certain group or cliques of parents; or because they're new in the school.
- Thank family members privately and publicly for providing resources or helping in other ways, showing appreciation in conversation, notes, homemade certificates of appreciation, and Family Homework, or with flowers or plaques. When Kathy and Ashley's grandmother, Dora Cruz, printed all of our homemade books, we honored her with a plaque at a Family Celebration.
- Try to get to know the families. Show real concern about their struggles and difficulties as well as their successes.
- Be determined to find ways to overcome problems so that you can have a positive relationship.
- Don't assume that just because a previous teacher didn't like a family member, you'll feel the same way. I set such information aside and try to make the relationship work. This doesn't always succeed, but over the past twenty-eight years I have learned to love and appreciate family members who were disliked by other teachers.
- Don't make assumptions about people's life experience, concern for their children, or the kind of person they are. People can really surprise you when you get to know them. Someone with a cold veneer may warm up to you. Give people the chance to surprise you.
- Be willing to reassess your own teaching when faced with a family member's comment or criticism.
- Be willing to be self-critical.

Find Ways to Communicate

From being a mother of three sons, the youngest of whom is a freshman in college, I know that most families feel locked out of their children's education. Unless we have a child who tells all, most parents don't know what goes on in our children's classrooms. We hardly know the topics of study, let alone the details.

Communicating with families is essential. We often get to see adults who deliver and pick up children, but we must always remember to reach out to families who don't come to school each day.

Communicate with Family Members Individually
- in the schoolyard or wherever children are dropped off in the morning or picked up in the afternoon
- through home visits
- by telephone
- with notes
- through e-mail
- in the classroom at a special conference or while the family member is helping out
- at social events such as lunch or dinner, concerts, plays, and celebrations

Communicate with All Families at Once Through
- letters
- newsletters
- surveys
- Family Homework
- phone calls or notes from volunteer class parent
- Curriculum Night, Back to School Night, and similar events
- Family Celebrations

Be Flexible

If we want family participation, we must be flexible about both the ways and the times they participate. We need to accommodate parents or grandparents who must bring babies or toddlers, and work around family members' schedules when they come to class for a specific project or activity. While I encourage people to come for interviews or quilting bees first thing in the morning, that's not always possible. We've had to arrange interviews or other activities for the late morning or the afternoon. With some family members, you can plan their participation way ahead of time. With others, like Ali's mother, Robin, their work schedules mean that you won't find out till the very last minute when they can come to class.

When a family member helps on a regular basis, I like them to be consistent so we can depend on them—the children are expecting them. Family members can help with research, reading, writing, or math. They typically help during specific times:

- every morning
- one morning, the same day, every week
- one day each month
- daily during Research Workshop, Center Time, or other special time
- once a week at Writing Workshop

Present Multiple Ways to Get Involved

Most of my class's family members are working or going to school, so I need to find many ways for them to be involved both in and outside of school. I need to think about family members who work full time or more, who are students, who have babies at home, or who have other circumstances that make participation difficult. Babies or toddlers often visit our classroom when their parents come to help. I use the Family Homework to suggest ways that families can get involved.

Families Are Vital Resources

In our inquiry classroom, families not only inform us about their children, but also provide human resources and material resources for our research studies.

Families Are a Valuable Human Resource

Families' life experiences are a primary source of information that goes way beyond the reach of any textbook because family members

- provide a range of perspectives
- portray the human aspects of the research topic
- serve as role models and teachers
- raise issues of morals and values
- enable the child or friend of the person being interviewed to feel great pride
- serve as a link to the community
- respond to our questions
- tell us their thoughts and information in ways that are accessible to young children

Because young researchers or children with disabilities may have limited reading skills, interviews or trips to family members' jobs sites are a great way to learn. You don't have to be a fluent reader or a great math thinker to learn from people. (You can read in detail about interviews in my book *Classroom Interviews: A World of Learning* [1998].)

Families Provide Material Resources

When I was a child, my home was filled with alternative newspapers, journals, books, and music, but my classroom had just the teacher and the single textbook. I determined that when I became a teacher, my classroom would be filled with myriad resources. In addition to providing a range of perspectives and human experience, families can share a wealth of material resources: books, news clippings, records and CDs, songs, stories, dances, and more.

Research studies change from year to year. Every year we reuse some of our accumulated resources, but we always need new ones. Most schools don't have the funds to purchase new resources each year, and we often don't have access to the same resources that families do. By reaching out to families for resources, we broaden the range of possible inquiry topics.

Families Can Shape a Research Study

The push for a particular topic may come from a family. In September, children wanted to do research about a singer and Ben's parents suggested that we select Woody Guthrie. I welcome such suggestions. In January when the children were making a new list of topics for future research, several children wanted to do research about health care workers because that's what their parents were.

We may not take up every one, but we generally try to incorporate family members' suggestions or questions into our study. Sometimes they offer a new perspective, which we welcome.

Families Can Get Involved Beyond the Classroom

Helping in the classroom is often the first step for a family member to get involved in schoolwide activities. I try to encourage their participation in Parent-Teacher Association (PTA) meetings, book fair planning and work, and other activities. The Notice section of the Family Homework shows how I inform families of possibilities for involvement outside of the classroom.

How does family involvement in schoolwide activities help my class? How does it help our research studies?

- Children often feel great pride and improved self-esteem when they see their family members involved in schoolwide activities.
- Involvement in schoolwide activities makes family members feel needed and important, which they are. Family members often tell me how schoolwide involvement has helped them build friendships and a support system that lasts for many years.

- While we work to push the city, state, and federal governments to provide more money for education, local fund-raising is essential. An active PTA can raise thousands of dollars for schoolwide improvements. At MNS, much of this money goes directly to the classrooms for books, maps, audio-visual equipment, and technology.
- Families who are involved in book fairs donate books that teachers want for our classrooms. Alumni families often purchase classroom books from the fair because they see the importance of books in the inquiry classroom.

Who Are the Class Families?

Because families play such an important role in our curriculum, I want to get to know about them quickly. Of course, some children had siblings in my previous classrooms, so I already know their families. Here are some of the ways I get information about families I don't know:

- I meet with the principal and the child's previous teachers.
- If the child has special needs, I meet with the child's school-based support team.
- I speak personally with families and ask questions, and I send home surveys that reflect our research studies. (See page 48 for an example.) The survey for an immigration study would ask about parents' and grandparents' country of origin, and whether they have contacts from parts of the world not represented in the class.

You can see from this survey that I try to respect families' privacy. If a parent doesn't want to tell about her job or the family's circumstances, that's fine.

After I gather the surveys, I collate the information on a chart, trying to memorize it.

Family Homework

Family Homework is a weekly packet of information and a few actual assignments that we use to inform families encourage their involvement in their child's education. It is a regular and consistent vehicle for empowering family members.

Combining Family Homework with personal contact can maximize family involvement. There are excerpts from the Family Homework of 1998–99 in the Appendix. The excerpts focus on the research studies that are in this book.

Many families are already quite involved with their children's education, but appreciate encouragement. They look forward to receiving the Family Homework

Social Studies Survey—Paula's class

During the year we will be doing research about People at Work. You, the families, are an important source of information about this topic. We value your participation in our thematic study.

(Please feel free to fill out only the parts of this survey you want.)

Name of your child _____

Type of work of mother or guardian _____

Type of work of father or guardian _____

Do you have any friends or neighbors whose work might be of interest to our class research about People at Work? _____

_____

Would any members of your family like to be interviewed about your job by our class in school or at your place of work?

_____

_____

Volunteer Survey—Paula's Class

__ Yes, I would like to help arrange class trips.

__ Yes, I have access to a copier and can make multiple copies of homemade books or other papers for the class.

__ Yes, I would like to help in the lunchroom and at recess.

__ Yes, I would like to help make a quilt about people we have interviewed for our study of People at Work.

__ Yes, I am available to help in the classroom.

Mondays __ Tuesdays __ Wednesdays __ Thursdays __ Fridays __

Please check areas of talent or interests you wish to share with our class:

__ arts and crafts   __ drama

__ sewing   __ dance

__ writing   __ science

__ storytelling   __ other _____

__ music (instrument or voice) _____

Adult signature X _____

Please return this survey as soon as possible.

© 2001 by Paula Rogovin from *The Research Workshop*. Portsmouth, NH: Heinemann on Monday evenings. Other families have little involvement with their children, but the Family Homework can help change that.

Family Homework Encourages Families to Help Their Children Learn

There's a healthy debate in many schools about whether we want families to help with homework. Some teachers are adamant that adults should not help with homework or projects. I deliberately call my homework *Family* Homework because I want families to help their children develop skills and understand concepts. I ask families to discuss issues with the children. Children benefit in so many ways when they see that their families really care how they do. This is not just theoretical: I have seen the evidence year after year.

Family Homework Provides a Great Opportunity to Integrate Social Studies and Other Subject Areas

While doing Family Homework, families sometimes find themselves dancing together, playing math games or solving problems, reciting poems, or doing a science experiment—activities that may be directly related to our research study.

Family Homework May Have Social Implications

While the Family Homework can improve academic skills, it also has social implications. The experiences that evolve from the Family Homework can last forever in a child's—or adult's—memory. The bonding, togetherness, and closeness that come from doing something together give children something positive to draw on in later life.

Family Homework Is a Tool for Planning and Assessment

Family Homework is a lot of work for me. I think about it in my car, at home in the evening or very early in the morning, when I should be sleeping, and during the weekend. Sunday morning is the time I actually sit down to prepare the Family Homework for the next week. Here's what I do:

- Evaluate what we have done.
- Assess each child's participation in class. Where there have been problems, I think of ways to improve things.
- Think about what is important to tell the families about last week's work in each curriculum area.
- Think about what issues or topics I want families to discuss with their children.

- Think about how to make our research study interdisciplinary. How can I bring science into our study? How can I connect it with literature? Is there any math in this? This helps me develop homework assignments and to project for the future in the classroom.
- Write about what we did in each curriculum area. This is one of the ways I document what we have done. *The Hundred Languages of Children* (Edwards, Gandini & Forman 1998) discusses the concept of documentation.
- Project what we'll do the next week in each curriculum area.
- Encourage family involvement. I ask families to discuss interviews, talk about specific issues, find more information about something, do specific experiments, play math games, and walk down the block and do specific observations.
- Develop assignments to emphasize concepts and develop skills.
- Try to be creative. Loris Malaguzzi wrote, "Our task, regarding creativity, is to help children climb their own mountains, as high as possible. No one can do more." (Edwards, Gandini & Forman 1998, 77)
- Create assignments that will develop the children's critical thinking skills. In the Family Homework you will often read comments such as: "talk about this together," or "think together about this." Sometimes I ask families to discuss something together and then I provide space for the child to draw or write about it. After telling about a book we read, I ask the families to think together about certain questions. After explaining that Chelsea's father told us that subway drivers are now called train operators rather than motormen, I ask the families to think together about how this change came about.

Family Homework Is a Preview of Things to Come

It's a good feeling for a parent to know that their child's teacher is thinking and planning activities all year. The activities give families something to look forward to—they can anticipate an interview or trip months in advance. Giving parents advance notice lets some of them take off from work or rearrange their schedules so they can attend.

How Can Families Help?

I want the families to help. For young children, the Family Homework is a kind of guided homework or guided at-home research. I often helped my own three sons with homework and projects when they were young. I want my students' families to

- set standards for their child's work. If the teacher's standards or expectations are higher than those of the parents, I want the families to raise their standards and help their child raise his standards. For example, if a parent or babysitter lets a child write sloppily, I will explain that the writing must be done in pencil, that it should be done neatly, that letters such as *b* or *d* that are reversed should be turned around, and that sentences must have capitals and end punctuation. I want the family to help the child apply this higher standard.

- discuss the child's school work with her
- explain things to the child when necessary
- show the child the possibilities for at-home assignments
- help the child develop research skills
- help the child present information in an interesting way

Children gradually become able to do homework and research projects on their own. This is what Stephanie Harvey calls "the gradual release of responsibility" (1998, 52).

Can Family Members Help Too Much?

Teachers often complain that parents are doing all the work. Some warn families to keep away. When I helped my own children with homework and projects, I was careful to let them do the bulk of the work. You can't expect a five- or six-year-old to do assignments on their own—they need some adult participation. It is urgent that you explain regularly to the families what you mean by "adult participation" and what you expect from the children and the family. I tell this to the families:

- Work together and discuss the homework.
- If there is a research project, do the research together.
- All writing must be in the children's handwriting.
- Unless I specifically ask family members to help, artwork must be done by the child. (Sometimes I do invite families to make additional drawings or objects.)
- I encourage them to find ways to make the work fun.

For reading assignments, I explain the strategies we use in school to figure out difficult words so that they can use those strategies at home. For writing assignments, I explain the use of approximated (invented) spelling and encourage them to let their children use it in first grade. More recently, for both reading and writing, I have encouraged families to make their own Word Wall of high-frequency words spelled in standard English. Each week I give them words to add, and I welcome them to add their own words to meet their children's needs.

When I asked families to help with a recycling project, I explained that I wanted them to make something—a vase, an animal, a pencil holder, or another object—

out of a plastic container, metal can, or Styrofoam egg carton. I told them that I wanted the whole family to help but to be sure the child did most of the work. I explained that I wanted them to talk about recycling, think together about what they would make, work together to gather materials, then do the project together. I emphasized that the children must do all of the writing.

When the projects came in, of course I could see the family influence. That was fine—in the process of doing the project, families had much positive interaction and fun together. Families and children alike were filled with pride from their successful shared experience.

Last year, unfortunately, one of the mothers did an entire research project for her child. It was easy to tell: The handwriting was not the child's and the information was presented in adult language. I spoke with the mother and the child, explaining again what I meant by family participation, and I set a date for their new project to be completed.

Probably more important than all of the skills learned in family projects is the communication between adults and children. Sometimes communication doesn't come easily; sometimes there are even battles. But when the child looks back, at the end of the school year or as an adult, he may appreciate the family help.

Special Family Projects

Each year we have short-term or yearlong projects that involve the families. Here are a few examples.

The People at Work Quilt

Early in 1998–99, I held a meeting of family members who wanted to work on a People at Work quilt. We met in the classroom before school. The parents had different ideas for how the quilt patches should be made. We decided to use different techniques:

- gluing fabric onto fabric patches
- using fabric crayons on fabric patches, then ironing the patches to make the colors stand out.

We then had a planning session with the children. We told the children that the patches would include pictures all of the people we had interviewed, our trips, and other information or issues from our research. We made a huge list of possibilities for the patches.

Figure 3–1. Tamiko Orasio and Ben Berkowitz's mother, Monique, at a quilting bee.

Work on the quilt went on all year, both at home and in school. At home, parents planned over the phone, purchased cloth for the background, and sewed pieces together. In school, during quilting bees, the parents helped children use the iron, and helped and encouraged children who were struggling with cutting, gluing, or coloring on fabric.

A Class Picture

Several parents and the children got together secretly to make a class-picture quilt. A parent coordinator transferred photographs onto cloth with the computer. A few parents worked with the children as they used watercolor crayons to color the photographs. The parent coordinator applied water with a paintbrush and stitched the patches together at home. At the end of the year, the parents surprised me by presenting me with an exquisite framed quilt of all the children's faces.

Celebrations

What are your special memories from school? For many people, the list is short. Others remember plays, family gatherings, sports, and other events. I want to give my students and their families such special memories.

We celebrate often in our inquiry classroom. Families usually bring food for these events. I always say that our classroom is not so good for people on diets! We have all kinds of parties and celebrations, including

- Breakfast parties to say good-bye to student teachers or other special people. These parties are often much easier for working parents to attend than events held immediately after school are.
- Parties to welcome special guests, like Woody Guthrie's daughter Nora. These parties take place when we do an interview, and sometimes family members are able to attend the interview and the party.
- Birthday parties. These are at 2:00 P.M. during Center Time and are rather low-key. Families bring cupcakes.
- Family Celebrations

What Is a Family Celebration?

The Family Celebration is a celebration of our research. Children present songs, dances, poetry, or a play—often created by the children or their families—related to our research studies. After the program we have a feast created by the families, student teachers, volunteers, and me. Family Celebrations usually involve 125 to 150 people.

During the celebration, guests see the classroom and halls, which are filled with the murals, dioramas, pictures, posters, photos, homemade movies, and other projects that have evolved from our inquiry studies. They cannot miss the themes of our research. The spirit of inquiry fills the air.

Why Have Family Celebrations? After our Family Celebration in November, I wrote this list of reasons to discuss with my student teachers because I wanted so much for them to help create lifelong memories for their future classes. We have Family Celebrations to

- celebrate our learning and our accomplishments
- celebrate research and inquiry
- have a culminating event for research studies
- build self-esteem

- develop acting, singing, and speaking skills
- develop bonds among families. Celebrations let families get better acquainted with each other. Some end up making friends, then supporting each other through shared babysitting, play dates, and other arrangements. An emotional support system often develops among families, too.
- give extended families, babysitters, and friends the chance to participate
- taste foods from different cultures
- build unity within the class
- create lifelong memories

Family Celebrations help build and strengthen the bond between school and family. I hope that the bonds we create will last well beyond the school year, and often they do.

How Do We Prepare for a Family Celebration? Getting ready for a Family Celebration is a big deal. These are major events that take a few months of preparation. I schedule celebrations months in advance so family members can reserve the date and I can clear it with my colleagues. An early start gives us time to create the program and rehearse.

What Are the Details? Family Celebrations are held from 5:30–7:30 P.M. so that family members who work during the day will be able to attend. We have celebrations twice a year, in late November or early December and in late May or early June.

The families and I prepare a potluck meal, which we place on tables in the hallway outside the classroom. We have separate tables for cups, plates, and plastic silverware; main dishes and salads; desserts; and drinks.

A setup committee of family members arrives at 5:00. Guests, including parents, grandparents, other relatives, babysitters, and family friends, arrive at 5:30. They remain in the classroom, hallway, and auditorium, looking at the children's work and mingling with each other. At 6:00 the program begins in the auditorium. After the program, everyone lines up to get food, then we eat in the classroom, hallway, and auditorium. The cleanup committee begins work at 7:30.

About a month before the Family Celebration, I send home a sheet of paper asking

How many people will attend from your family?
Which food will your family bring—salad, main dish, dessert?
Can you help with the setup or cleanup committee?

What Are the Secrets for a Successful Family Celebration? There are some "tricks of the trade" that can make preparing for these major events much easier:

- Do not let families sign up to bring paper goods or juice. A new teacher once did that and had only napkins and juice to serve! I purchase those things myself as my contribution, or I speak to families on the side and ask them to bring those things.
- Notify families in writing at least a month in advance, then remind them repeatedly.
- Have a few family members call all of the families as a reminder. There might be someone who didn't read the weekly reminders in the Family Homework, and you don't want a child to miss the celebration.
- If a family isn't planning to attend, speak to them personally to encourage them to participate. If they can't, suggest that they send their child with a relative or friend, or another family from the class. Because the Family Celebration is a whole-class event, it is essential that every child attend. The presence of a family member makes children feel supported.
- Practice, practice, and practice. Start early. You may have to make big scheduling changes, but you really need to practice. The children should be able to get on and off the stage and do their presentation with little or no assistance from the teacher. If you rehearse a lot, the children will be able to focus not on where and how to stand, but on the quality of the presentation.

A Parent Speaks Out

Sam's mother, Miriam, wrote this poem. The train whistle she refers to is one I bought at a coal mine in Pennsylvania. Every morning, I gather the children together in the schoolyard by blowing that whistle, which makes them feel as if we are going on an adventure—and we are. Miriam read her poem at a holiday breakfast on December 22, 1998. I must say that I feel the same way about the families. Tears flowed at that beautiful gathering.

Ode/Ode to Paula
Miriam Herscher
Paula, we know that poems touch your heart
And so for today, we shall do our part

For you, we come to celebrate
As a teacher you are surely and truly great
We are luckier by far than you'll ever know
To have you nurture our children and help them to grow

On the first day of school you invited us all in
I sang "This land is your land" with a wonderful grin
To be partners with you in this marvelous feat . . .
I knew then and there we were in for a treat

You value our children and their inquiring minds
You allow them choice and encourage their own ways to find
Your passion and values set you apart
You have a gentle yet firm manner and teach with all your heart

You work with developmental issues in an incredible way
The child is never wrong, we can almost hear you say
You go for their strengths and cheer them on their way
We wish we had your patience and always the right thing to say

You teach about the past, instilling values and humility
You are one remarkable woman with exceptional ability
You greet every morning with a smile and the gentle whistle of a
    train
You remind us all daily of how much we and our children have
    to gain

You inspire us and we are in awe in no small measure
You are clearly and truly a teaching treasure
As the years go by we will all remember
How lucky we felt from the first day of September

In gratitude, and always mindful of your generous spirit
We thank you, Paula, with all our heart and soul
And we know you can hear it!

4

Our Inquiry Classroom: The Room Itself

Our Classroom

Room 407 is in a building that is nearly one hundred years old. Girls and boys came into school through separate entrances. One of my classes learned that in the old days the desks in Room 407 were in rows and were bolted to the floor. The desks are gone, replaced by work tables, and the room has a carpet and interesting nooks and crannies. The signs for the separate entrances to the school remain but are ignored.

I hope that Room 407 embodies the principles of my teaching. I want it to be a place where children conducting research studies have easy access to resources. I want it to be comfortable for the children, their families, student teachers, and me.

Our Classroom Reflects Our Research Studies

Our classroom and the surrounding halls are filled with the spirit of our research. When you walk into our room, you know something special is going on: It is a content-rich environment, and you can feel it. If you return to our room in a week, a month, or several months, you'll feel and see that our research has evolved. You'll see evidence of new topics and more sophisticated writing, reading, and art, and you'll hear more sophisticated and more animated discussions.

In *Nonfiction Matters* (1998), Stephanie Harvey says,

> Walls can teach . . . Halls offer the open space environmentalists dream of. Use the halls to your advantage . . . Halls come alive when we see the tracks of the students who inhabit them. (43)

Our Classroom Is Multicultural and Reflects Concern About Gender Issues

Our classroom is multicultural: I make every effort to have representations of different races, cultures, and nationalities and to be sure that the books, poems, drawings, paintings, photos, crayons, paint, markers, and other resources reflect the diversity of humanity. I make every effort to reflect diversity and raise gender issues within the curriculum rather than as an add-on.

Access

I remember as a child sitting with my hands folded, waiting to hang up my coat or for supplies to be passed out. Oh, did we waste a lot of time waiting and being quiet as we waited. It's not just the time we wasted that upsets me now as I think back, it's the lack of confidence this ritual implies. Why can't children get their own journals? Why can't a child go over to the paper supply alone and take what she needs? Why can't a child walk to the boxes of writing folders and get her own folder for Writing Workshop?

I love the hum of an inquiry classroom. Resources for our research studies are accessible to the children because this is their classroom. Children are empowered to hang up their coats and get their supplies and books by themselves. When I first arrived at MNS six years ago, our principal, Shelley Harwayne, told us not to do anything for the children that they can do for themselves. Of course a child can select her own materials. Certainly children can bring research materials to Research Workshop each day. There's no doubt that children can get their own folders for Writing Workshop. Doing things on their own makes children feel good about themselves because they know that the teacher trusts them.

A Quick Tour

A quick tour of our classroom and a few photos will help you understand what I mean by accessibility.

Shelves, Cabinets, and Baskets

One set of shelves was discarded by another teacher. Another is an old cubby turned sideways. There's nothing fancy, just a bunch of miscellaneous shelves, cabinets, and baskets that hold the resources for our research—books, magazines, pictures, records, CDs, tapes, and more.

There's a rack where we display books that we have read recently. Children who have completed their work can grab books from this rack.

Sections of Resources. There are several sections of resources, each with a label:

Fiction
Folktales and Fairy Tales
Poetry
Books with Math (often fiction)
Songs and Games
Science
Books for Our Reading Workshop
Social Studies
Records
Videos

Special Sections for Each Inquiry Study. Once the children have selected their research topics, we set up a special place to keep the resources for each topic. I may write labels for these special collections in the beginning of the year, but later in the year you will see only child-made labels.

At the beginning of a study the shelves may hold only a few items. As the families, my colleagues, and friends send things in and the student teachers and I gather other materials, the shelves fill up.

Once research topics are set, I comb through the entire classroom library for books that would be appropriate for each topic. It's a big challenge to find fiction, music, and poetry related to our topics. Books from different sections end up in our special research collections. After a few days of work within a research group, the children know just where to go to find these materials.

In *Nonfiction Matters* (1998), Stephanie Harvey calls these special collections *text sets* and discusses various types of them. Text sets can be organized around unit studies, individual studies, social issues, and other topics. In my classroom children are less involved in grouping resources than older children are.

Placement of Resources is Strategic

Classroom arrangements may look spontaneous, but they're really well thought-out. Placing resources for a research group is strategic. For example, Amber's sports research group kept books and other materials on a table just below a mural they made, right near where the children line up for lunch or dismissal so they could look at the bats, balls, and books while they were waiting in line.

The books about coal and steel for the vehicle research group were on a cabinet top near our coal mine in the block area, just waiting for someone to stop to look at them while they were working in the coal mine. Later in the year, when the block

Figure 4–1. Chelsea Grant in front of the special collection of resources for the Woody Guthrie research group.

area became a hospital, we replaced the coal and steel books with books and resources about health care workers.

The books, articles, song sheets, and photographs for our Woody Guthrie research were together on a shelf labeled "Woody Guthrie." This section was next to the carpet where we have story circle, so we could grab a book with a Woody Guthrie song or reach for *This Land Is Your Land* if we wanted to explain our research to a guest.

The Paint Area

There's lots of research-related painting in our classroom. A custodian attached some wallboard to a wall for us. It's tucked behind the block area. I wish the room were much bigger, but we have produced hundreds of murals in this tiny space. A sign on the mural wall says *"Mural in Progress,"* and there is always a mural in some stage of production. We move finished murals to another spot in the room or out in the hallway.

We have paints of many colors, including brown, which many schools do not supply. I have developed expertise in mixing many shades of brown so that the children can represent the many shades of people in the world.

Mural Displays

Because I want us to literally be surrounded by our research, we have figured out a number of ways to display our work. We hang our murals at and above standard bulletin board level. Some murals hang from a clothesline, and some from a mural holder I designed and the custodian was kind enough to install. It's an old window pole that hangs in front of our windows. I hooked clips onto the rod and we hang our butcher paper murals from two of the clips.

This arrangement gives us many places to display murals from each research group. Some murals stay up in the classroom all year. When we made a mural of Woody Guthrie giving his coat to a stranger, I wanted the children to see it over and over so they would remember it. We hang other murals on bulletin boards in the hallway to share our research with the whole school. After some murals have been displayed for a while we fold them and save them for the end of the year, when the children take all of the murals home. You can find out more about how we use the finished murals in Chapter 6.

Figure 4–2. The mural about the working conditions of farm workers who pick strawberries is hanging from a specially designed mural hanger.

Figure 4–3. Cabinet doors with information about the interviews of Chelsea Grant's father, Stephan, and Samuel Herscher's uncle, David.

Walls, Door Panels, and Cabinet Backs

Research groups are given sections of the bulletin board on which to display their work and photographs, drawings, paintings, collages, word webs, and other projects related to interviews. Projects may also be taped to the doors or backs of cabinets. These documents enable children and adults to return to earlier topics, and even to add to what they did before. They also enhance our memories. Often during an interview or a discussion, children will point to a mural, a poster, or a word web. They know I love it when they do that.

The Block Area

Sometimes during Center Time the children build whatever they want in the block area. But we also use the block area for our research. It has been a construction site, the Chunnel between France and England, and other places. It's a lively area for both girls and boys. In 1998–99, the block area was a coal mine, then a hospital, with all of the appropriate paraphernalia. The mine had hard hats, plastic railroad tracks and trains, real anthracite coal and other rocks, lanterns, and more. The hospital had real gowns, stethoscopes, bandages, hats, face masks, dolls, a homemade blood bank, real X-ray film, a box with fake medical records, and more. Most of the items were sent in by the families.

Computers

One of our two computers is connected to the Internet. That is our research computer. The children use the Internet to look at maps, consult with experts about their topics, e-mail people, watch videos, look at photographs from the Library of Congress, and much more, all with adult supervision. They also work independently at the computers to do word processing or play educational games.

The Writing Center

This Writing Center cabinet has shelves for different kinds and sizes of paper. Some of the paper is blank, and some is special writing paper I designed on the computer. One type of the special writing paper has blank space at the top for pictures, with five lines below. Another type has blank space and ten lines. Still another has paper filled with lines. Children have free access to the paper, with rules limiting how much they can take at one time. They also have access to staplers in this center.

The Word Wall

The Word Wall is a large alphabet chart. I write words onto index cards using large print, which makes them easier to see. The colored markers I use have no particular meaning, but make it easy for a child to look for "the purple word under the letter g" or "the red word under the w." The children refer to the Word Wall frequently.

The Math Area

The math area has a mobile cabinet with sections for manipulatives. Large containers hold attribute blocks, Cuisenaire rods, geoblocks, and pattern blocks. Children use these materials during Math Workshop and have access to them at Center

Figure 4–4. This part of our Word Wall has a combination of high-frequency words and key words from our research study. Many of the words here are a reflection of the research about health care workers, scientists, and garment workers.

Time. Children often use the math manipulatives to build things or solve problems connected to our research studies.

Work Tables

Some of our work tables are hexagonal (actually two trapezoids pushed together); some are round. Each table holds containers of pencils and erasers, colored pencils, water-based markers and crayons, and a vase with flowers. In the beginning of the year I ask families to donate supplies. Some supplies come from the school. All of the supplies on the tables are shared. We have no private pencils or markers. This makes life in the classroom much more peaceful and democratic.

Story Circle

Story Circle is a large carpet where we gather for whole-class activities. It's my favorite place to sit for Research Workshop because there's room for role-plays. We

Figure 4–5. Paula and the class singing at Story Circle during Meeting.

have a large rocking chair that we use for our classroom interviews. Sometimes we sit in a circle. Other times my student teacher or I sit in the rocking chair and the children, as they say, "sit in a bunch."

Maps

We have a map ritual. Nearly every time someone mentions a country or part of the U.S., we look at our wall maps and touch that place with a long pointer. The maps hang behind the rocking chair. Near the commercial maps is a map that the children painted of the Caribbean Islands. That one helps us identify the locations of poems we love by Monica Gunning (from Jamaica) and Lynn Joseph (from Trinidad). We also have a box of maps that children can use to get a closer look. These maps can be added to the resources for a particular research study.

We have maps of all regions of the world. Because we use our maps so much, there's a lot of "map talk" in our room, and by mid-year the can children point to locations on the map without any teacher involvement.

The Science Area

The science area is home to our science library and our various pets. In 1998–99 we had a rabbit, snails, slugs and other garden animals, and toads. Children take the animals out at Center Time alone or in small groups. During Writing Workshop, children take a clipboard and do observations of an animal.

Cubbies, Writing Containers, and Mailboxes

This very old school building has built-in oak storage areas that we have turned into cubbies where children store their journals and other work. If we didn't have these cubbies, I would buy rubber or plastic boxes to give the children space for their materials. Above the cubbies are four color-coded containers that hold the children's writing folders, which are color-coded to match the containers. The color-coding has nothing to do with the children's academic ability—it just makes it easy for them to find or return their writing folders by themselves.

Last year was the first time we had a mailbox with a section for each child. It was a commercially built container, but could easily have been homemade from boxes. Children put their homework folders in the mailbox every day, and we put notices and work to be returned there, too.

These various cubbies and containers help the children be more independent. And because I don't have to pass out or collect things all the time, they help speed things up, too.

The Landfill

Our "landfill" is a soil-filled milk crate in which we bury bottles, cans, newspaper, Styrofoam, and fruits and vegetables, with worms added to the mix. We use the landfill for our study of recycling, digging things up and observing changes through the year.

The Dress-Up Area

Our dress-up area is two large plastic containers that are filled with donated clothing that is great for role-play. The clothes, along with all kinds of work hats, are a Center Time favorite. Dress-up scenarios are often related to our research studies.

Spaces That Are Off-Limits to the Children

There are just a few spaces in the classroom that are off-limits to the children—a container of permanent markers, the adults' coat closet, and a supply cabinet that holds hammers, nails, saws, and other such materials. Children need permission to go into these areas.

The Hallway

At Manhattan New School the hallways are considered work areas, an extension of our classrooms. Hallways are furnished with tables and chairs, often painted with colorful designs. I feel comfortable sending two or three children out to the hall to work on a project or discuss an issue. For safety reasons, children need my permission to work in the hallway.

Dealing with Problems

In nearly every class, there are a few children—the bumpers and the pokers—who need ongoing work to make getting supplies a peaceful event. In every community people need to learn to cooperate, to work together. In our class, we talk about rituals for getting supplies and for navigating transitions. When there are problems, we approach them as we do our research studies. We ask questions and search for solutions. Some violations of our code of conduct result in a time-out or a talk with the child's family.

Cleanup

We live in our room together and children have easy access to nearly everything. With that freedom of access comes the responsibility for cleanup. Time for cleanup is built into each workshop and Center Time. I'm quick to compliment children who take the initiative to clean up without being told. Children love to be complimented, so soon there are lots of children who take that initiative. After a while, many children help automatically. Family members are often shocked at how well their children help at school—at home it's usually another story.

Summary

As the children learn to become more independent, I love to stand back and watch. In the morning as they hang their coats in the closet, put homework folders in the mailbox, put chairs back at the tables, get research journals from their cubbies, bring materials to the research group, and chat with their friends along the way, I smile with pride at how well they accomplish their tasks. The children and I know that *of course* they can do it.

5

Writing in Our Inquiry Classroom

An Inquiry Classroom Is a Spawning Ground for Writers

An inquiry classroom is a content-rich environment that gives children plenty to think and write about. It is a real spawning ground for writers.

Writing Is Developmental

My approach to inquiry is developmental, and so is my approach to teaching children to become writers. I start by assuming that every child—whether he writes with pictures or she is fluent writing with words—is a writer. All are equal in my eyes. We celebrate each child's ability to record thoughts and information by whatever means possible. If a child is in the drawing stage, that's his most important tool for recording information. If teachers honor that ability, however developed or undeveloped it is, the child will become comfortable with writing.

My philosophy is not "I teach; the children learn and apply the learning." Rather, it's "We begin with the tools the children have." As we introduce new skills, the children approximate them at their own pace. In writing, we call this approximated writing or invented spelling. I may introduce the concept of using a period at the end of a sentence in October. Some children will put periods in their writing that same day. Others may not put periods in their writing independently until December or March, after months of reviewing and practicing the concept.

In an inquiry classroom, the children become each other's teachers. We all move forward, whether at a snail's pace or at the speed of lightning. The non-judgmental interaction we promote moves everyone forward as writers.

There Are Many Tools for Writing

Our inquiry classroom uses many of the same tools and techniques that other classrooms use for Writing Workshop. One difference is that in an inquiry classroom there is ongoing research, so there are always new topics and issues to write about and new vocabulary words to use. (I call them *key words*.) We use many tools to write.

Pictures

Pictures are welcome. They can be very informative, and I encourage that. In October when children were recording in their journals about how rubber is made for use in cars, they drew pictures of the latex flowing from the tree. Some of the drawings had precise details; others were sprawled across the page, their content nearly unrecognizable. Both types were okay. Both were praiseworthy.

Approximated or Invented Spelling

Writing happens throughout the day, starting the first day of school. The children gradually move from pictures to approximated spelling to standard English. With approximated spelling, the children write whatever they think represents the sounds they hear. During Reading Workshop in the beginning of the year, we often practice sounding out words from our homemade books, stretching them to hear each sound. For some words, like *hat* or *sit*, that's easy. However, if there are letters that don't make any sound, I just add them to the word. In the word *teach*, as we stretch the word, early spellers will say that they hear the *t* and *e* and the *ch*. As they say that, I print *teach* so they can write *teach* in its standard English spelling in their journals. I may invent a silly story about why the *a* is silent when it's hanging out with the *e* as a way of introducing the *ea* spelling. If part of a word can't be sounded out through stretching, I just write those letters. So, if children predict that the word *beautiful* will be in a book, early spellers will hear the *b, t, i, f,* and *l.* I add the other letters as I write on the board and explain that this word comes from the French language so we keep some of the French spelling. Little by little we introduce spelling concepts or language issues. This word study during Reading Workshop helps the children with both reading and writing.

During Research Workshop, Writing Workshop, and while children write homemade books, adults work with individual children to sound out words. The children write only the sounds they hear or know. For example, if an early writer writes *ht* for the word *hat*, *bg* for *big*, or *st* for *sit*, it's probably an indication he doesn't know some of the vowel sounds yet. That's okay. If a child asks if the spelling is right, I say, "that's fine," or "great job."

One of the most exciting things about teaching young children is seeing writing skills fall into place over time. As they learn the sounds of letters, become readers, learn high-frequency words from the Word Wall, and learn to use environmental print, their writing gets closer and closer to standard English. To see children go from picture writing to writing poems, songs, multiple-page books, and interview journals filled to the brim is amazing.

As the children become more comfortable with writing, I introduce editing and revision skills. Gradually, they are expected to begin sentences with capital letters, add ending punctuation, and change approximated spelling to match that on the word wall, murals and signs or in their personal dictionaries in their writing folders. I teach them strategies for revising their work such as finding a word to replace the word *nice*, providing more detail, or grabbing the reader's attention. For each child, that emphasis on editing and revision takes place at a different point in the year.

High-Frequency Words

High-frequency words are the ones that are used most in English, and sometimes they have odd or confusing spellings. It's a good idea to know how to spell or read these words without having to sound them out. The high-frequency words include *the, and, in, this, about,* and *around*. During guided reading, we emphasize these words early on so they will be internalized as soon as possible. As the year progresses, our high-frequency words get more difficult. We usually post high-frequency words on our Word Wall so children can refer to them as they write or read.

Key Words

Key words are words we are using for research studies. We write them in standard English, putting them on the board and adding them to our Word Wall as they come up during research. You can just imagine how much this helps children develop a more sophisticated vocabulary.

For example, when doing research about child labor, some of the key words were *child labor, children, pesticides,* and *wages*. While doing research about how steel is made, we did a role-play. Then I drew a picture on the board. The children helped me figure out letters to use to label the pictures. I added letters so each word would be in standard English: *coal, coke, iron ore, blast oven,* and so on. The children made their own pictures and labels in their journals, and I expected those labels to be in standard English, though the other words in their notes were in approximated spelling.

Handwriting

Writing is a tool for communication and documentation, so it must be legible and neat. In the beginning of the year, children approximate legibility. For some, the hand muscles are well-developed early on. Others need more practice. Early in the year we have handwriting lessons, practicing letter formation, spacing, and use of capital letters and punctuation. During reading or research I often model the formation of key or high-frequency words so the children will record them carefully in their journals. As the children's ability to form letters improves, my expectations get higher.

What Does the Writing Experience Look Like?

When children write in our classroom, the environment is their teacher. That's why we like to have a print-rich environment. Children write using a combination of pictures, approximated spelling, and high-frequency words and key words copied from the classroom environment, where those words might be on a chart, word web, mural, sign, label, or Word Wall. I remind the children explicitly and repeatedly that all these ways of getting assistance with writing are welcome. That frees them to feel comfortable with writing.

When children are writing in our classroom, they can do all of these things without permission:

- stand near the Word Wall to check for a particular word
- open the classroom door to check the spelling of the word *people* on the People at Work hallway sign
- walk over to our word web to find a word
- go over to the poetry collection to check the spelling of words in poems they know
- copy the names of their classmates from the cubbies or mailboxes
- stop at the shelf of books from our research studies to check the spellings
- bend to see the ordinal numbers chart, which is placed on the side of a cabinet low to the floor
- look for a color on the color chart or the days or months of the year on those charts
- check their journal, where they know they wrote the word
- search through a book they know has a word they need

You may have noticed that I didn't mention asking the teacher or a friend for spelling help. We have an expression in our class: "We don't do 'How do you spell.'" Once a teacher lets children use her to spell words, there's no end to the practice—

there will be a nonstop parade of children with "How do you spell's." Discouraging reliance on a teacher or classmate forces children to develop their research skills, so we help them develop their own strategies for spelling. They must either sound out the word or think of where they can get help from the classroom environment.

Opportunities for Writing in Our Inquiry Classroom

Actually writing is one of the best ways to become a fluent writer, so writing is built into our day.

Writing at Research Workshop

At Research Workshop we stop frequently for children to take notes. I prefer having all of the children record our observations, but will occasionally have a single person record. Some teachers appoint a child or get a volunteer to record information for the group. This practice varies depending on the age of the children and the teacher's goal. Why have children take notes?

- It gives them an opportunity to process information.
- It gives them a way to save information for future reference—it serves as a memory.
- Recording through pictures and letters develops fine motor skills.
- It enables them to practice reading and writing high-frequency and key words in standard English.
- It lets them practice using approximated spelling.
- The lines in the journals encourage them to move from left to right and from top to bottom on the page.

Children bring their research journal to Research Workshop. After we have observed or discussed something important, I ask them to write about it. Sometimes we review the information briefly before they write. We sometimes construct a diagram on the board, and the children copy it, adding their own personal touches. The adults write key words on the board so the children can use those words as they write. I often remind the children that a word they need is on the Word Wall. If there's no resource for a particular word, the children use approximated spelling.

When the children were recording information about rubber production, our student teacher, Karen Dunlap, wrote key words on the board: *tree*, *pail*, *latex*. The children helped her figure out the letters, and she added letters so the words would be in standard English. The children copied the words. This approach honors where the children are while moving them forward into standard spelling.

As they become more fluent writers, many children don't need to be reminded to take notes. They can't wait to show me or any other adult their marvelous accomplishment.

We observe children as they write and help them when necessary. We often ask children to share what they have written or to hold it up so others can see. We praise the work of fluent writers and of those who are working hard but may still be struggling to record information.

Children in a research group often work together to write a book, big book, play, or skit as they complete their formal research. This is their opportunity to share their work or to move from inquiry to social action.

Writing at Writing Workshop

Writing Workshop is a favorite time of day in our classroom. After several years of noisy Writing Workshops, I decided to transform them into a calm and quiet time. In the noisy workshops there was low productivity and lots of socializing, and children relied heavily on each other for spelling. Now, unless children are collaborating on a piece, sharing a published piece, or working with an adult, there's no talking.

All through the year we work with different genres during Writing Workshop—poetry, folktales and fairy tales, fiction, nonfiction, plays, and songs. Sometimes we will have a poetry study for several weeks. Exposing children to different genres of writing during Research Workshop, Meeting, and Writing Workshop opens up many possibilities for expression.

At Writing Workshop children determine their own topics. They can work on stories or nonfiction writing for a day, a month, or longer. Stories at the beginning of the year tend to be about family, "my day," or trips to the park. But as the research studies evolve, the topics expand.

If a child is trying to think of a new topic for a book, I might say, "Let's try to think of something from your research group." She might even choose to write about another group's findings. Some of our greatest poetry, stories, and nonfiction at Writing Workshop comes from children looking at the notes in their research or interview journals or glancing around the room at the murals and bulletin boards. Writing about our research studies is catchy. If the adults make a big deal about the fact that a child wrote about a research topic, there will certainly be another child who will do the same the next day.

Writing at Reading Workshop and Math Workshop

At Reading Workshop, children take notes. At Math Workshop, they take notes, write observations, and write about their math thinking or solutions to problems.

Writing at Meeting

Many a song or poem has been composed by the whole class at Meeting. As children suggest words, I hurriedly jot them down. We do some revision together, then I revise further at another time during the day with a few children or alone at home. So often these songs and poems are related to our research studies.

Writing at Interviews

During interviews I stop periodically for the children to take notes. With new writers, I must provide a lot of scaffolding: We review the topic briefly and I ask for suggestions for ways to write about it. I remind the children that they can write with pictures or words. Sometimes I ask children to hold up their journals so others will see how they represented information or concepts. We compliment pictures and other representations. When children see others using print, they usually push themselves to use print. That's one great advantage of heterogeneous grouping—the children become each other's teachers.

As the children become more comfortable with approximated spelling, I urge them to write with words. By January or February, many have made the transition, and the number of pictures is reduced drastically. (See Figure 5–1 on the following page.)

Writing Homemade Books

Shortly after an interview or trip, children write a page for a homemade book. (We don't do this during Writing Workshop, because that's when children choose their own topics.) After an interview, we have a brief discussion about the topics that can go into our homemade book. Children select paper with a few or many lines. While they write, adults circulate among them to help with content and actual writing. After they have written, I work with them to edit. The degree of editing we do depends on where each child is in his development.

Writing Signs and Labels

The documentation of our research and other work always has a label. Children put labels next to the photographs we have taken in the room or on trips, on our murals, and on bulletin board displays. They love to make signs in the block area.

In the beginning of first grade, the children write signs in approximated spelling, then an adult rewrites the words in standard English below the children's writing, using a marker. Both invented and standard spellings are displayed. As the year progresses and children's writing becomes more fluent, they edit their signs and labels. We go over their final edit with a marker so it will be more visible.

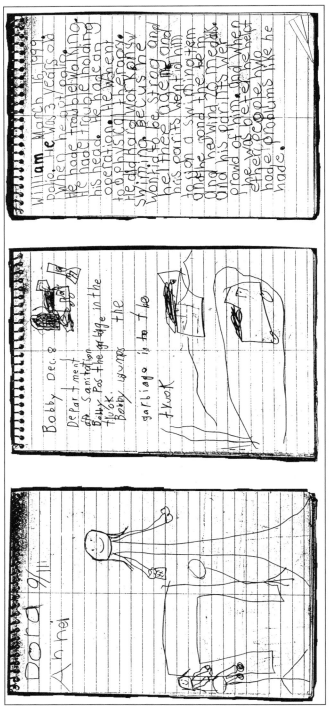

Figure 5–1. Annelise Stabenau's notes from her interview journal—September 11, December 8, and March 16.

76

Writing signs and labels serves several purposes:

- The children practice writing. They practice forming the letters, making spaces, adding punctuation, and going from left to right and from top to bottom.
- They practice using environmental print.
- They practice reading.
- The children feel so proud when they see their writing posted in the class-room or hallways.
- The children look at the signs and remember their earlier experiences.
- Other people entering the classroom or hallway find out what we are doing. They often make a comment or ask a relevant question. This not only helps the children review the topic and deepen their understanding, but gives them great pride. For example:

> "Oh, Ashley, your father made this stone carving. Wow, he's really great!"
>
> "You met Brian Pinkney! I love his work. Please tell me about him."
>
> "I saw your bulletin board about Elizabeth Blackwell. Did you know that my mother wasn't allowed to become a doctor just because she was a woman?"

Writing Letters

Because we interact with so many people during our research studies, we are always writing letters. The adults model a letter-writing format and in the beginning of the year the children approximate that format. Children write both handwritten and e-mail letters of inquiry and thanks. They sometimes even write a letter of advocacy to the mayor, the president, or other officials. Because of our concern about social development, children have also written letters of apology to others they may have offended.

Writing at Home

Nearly every Family Homework assignment involves writing, whether it is for reading, social studies, science, or math.

Recording Information from Our Research Studies

We have found lots of ways to record information from our research studies. Some ways, such as journals, are for the children's personal use. Other ways, such as videos, murals, and photographs, are meant to be shared with the families and the larger community.

Journals

In my earlier years of research studies we used sheets of lined paper to record information. The children put the papers in their cubbies or into folders, and it was a grand mess. I vowed never to use loose sheets again. Research journals are a must for several reasons:

- They house notes from day to day and the work stays in one place.
- They make it possible to keep work in sequence.
- Because they are manageable, they empower children to be in charge of their own work. The children know where to record new information. They can find work from previous days and refer back to their notes.
- They provide a tool for assessment. When the children first arrive at Research Workshop, they copy the date from the board or calendar into their research journals, which helps us use the journals for assessment. At a family conference we may look at a child's journal to see what kind of work she was doing in September, January, or May. When did the child use invented spelling? At what point did the child become more focused? Children love to look back at their earlier notes and marvel at how they have improved.

What Kinds of Journals Do We Use? Over the years I have found that certain notebooks work better than others. I buy them for the whole class (and get reimbursed by the school or the PTA) so that everyone has the same type of journal. Office supply stores often sell notebooks in bulk or offer discounts on them in late summer and early September. (I have bought one-subject notebooks for as little as twenty-five cents.) We don't decorate our covers, but some classes do. Here are my recommendations:

- *Interview journals*   Our interview journals are steno pads. They are exclusively for interviews in the classroom. We don't ever take them on trips because they are so valuable and we can't risk losing them. One year a parent who was a journalist ordered reporter's notebooks for each child. These notebooks fit in a pocket. We used them for trips.
- *Spiral notebooks*   We use one-subject spiral notebooks with wide lines. The children have separate journals for Research Workshop (blue), Reading Workshop (purple), and Math Workshop (green).

Hardcover "marble" notebooks work well, too, especially for children who have a habit of playing with the metal spiral of the spiral notebooks. The whole binding can fall apart, though, if children rip pages out.

Family Involvement

Since families are such an important part of our research, it's crucial for them to know about the children's experiences with writing in the classroom. Family members at MNS learn about approximated spelling when their children are in kindergarten. In first grade, they learn even more about it when they come to help in the room, at family conferences, at curriculum night, and in the Family Homework. In the Appendix you will see numerous examples of family involvement in the writing process in the excerpts from the Family Homework of February 1, March 8, and March 22.

Because most family members learned to write using a more traditional approach, some may find it difficult or impossible to accept the developmental approach that allows the use of approximated spelling. But when we take the time to inform them about approximated spelling, they usually support the effort at home.

Summary

In our research studies we make every effort to bring the world into our classroom. This content-rich environment gives the children a world of topics and opportunities for their writing. Writing is both for children's personal use and a means to share their inquiry with the world.

6

Literature and Reading in Our Inquiry Classroom

The use of literature and the teaching of reading are integral parts of an inquiry classroom. Both will be discussed in this chapter.

The Use of Literature

Quality literature plays a huge part in our inquiry classroom. Here are some of the questions about literature that we will explore in this chapter.

- What is quality literature?
- How does literature enhance a research study?
- What kinds of literature can we use?
- How do we know which book would "fit," or even which books are out there?
- Where can a teacher, particularly a new teacher, find quality literature?

What Is Quality Literature?

In her book *Lasting Impressions* (1992), Shelley Harwayne talks about rich texts that have layers of meaning and will "more likely lead to a rich variety of personal responses" (62). She writes

> We've not only come to appreciate that responding to literature can help students find their own topics for writing, we've come to value literature as a major resource for generating topics. (61)

I think of quality children's literature in these ways:

- If there is a message, the author doesn't smack the readers on the head with it, but tells it in an artistic or subtle way.

- The book, whether in standard English or in a dialect or vernacular, is effective in developing an idea, message, or story.
- The language enriches our lives.
- The characters, whether people or animals, have some depth.
- If there are illustrations, they match and enhance the text.
- Some fantastic picture books have elements of science, the arts, social studies, and even mathematics. In *Goodnight Moon*, by Margaret Wise Brown, the green on the wall gets darker and muddier as it gets later in the night, so it's a great book for teaching about the effect of light on color. And while Leo Lionni, John Steptoe, and Vera B. Williams' books tell us stories, they also teach us about human values.
- Quality literature pushes our thinking.
- Quality literature teaches about things or issues.
- Some quality literature subtly teaches us about the human condition through characters who are animals, not people.
- Quality literature inspires us to write and gives us topics to write about.

Don't be fooled. Some books are so physically attractive that they look like quality literature when they aren't. Yes, there are books that have all the "right" things—stories about people of different races or nationalities, beautiful pictures, rich colors, or gorgeous covers. But so often the writing is dull, unimaginative, and stiff.

Some words of caution: Always preview a book before you read it to your class. It may be someone else's favorite but not right for you or your class. When my three sons were young, I read every book to them before I read it to my class and they told me if it was a good book or not. We discussed their reasoning. Generally I agreed with them, and if they didn't like a book, I usually didn't read it to my class. I feel happy that they got to hear so many books.

How Does Literature Enhance Research Study?

At afternoon Meeting, I read *Nobody Owns the Sky: The Story of "Brave Bessie" Coleman*, by Reeve Lindbergh (1996). The children were spellbound as my voice traveled up and down along the story line, which is told in rhyme. The children listened intently as they anticipated the rhymes. What a delightful way to learn about Bessie Coleman, the first woman pilot in the United States.

"That sounds like Jackie Robinson," said a child.

"Why?" I asked.

"Well, he was brave, and he didn't let anyone stop him," he replied.

"People were mean to Bessie Coleman, and they were mean to Jackie Robinson," answered another.

"It was hard for Bessie because she was a woman and she was black. They really didn't like that!"

A hand waved frantically to get my attention. "That's like Elizabeth Blackwell."

"What do you mean?" I asked.

"Nobody would let her go to those medical schools."

"It's like Wilma Rudolph, too."

"Do you know anyone in your lives who is like that, too?" I asked.

The conversation continued as children offered a wonderful blend of ideas garnered from their research groups, interviews, and literature we had read. The discussion was a glorious collage of bravery, of people who struggled to overcome obstacles and were triumphant.

That morning in the athletes research group, our student teacher, Amber Frantz, had read more details from a book about Jackie Robinson. After recording the details in their research journals, the children did a few quick role-plays. At Share Time they told the class what they had learned. At Meeting that afternoon, a child was quick to tell me why I read *Nobody Owns the Sky*.

"I know why you read that book, Paula."

"Why?" I asked innocently.

"Cause it's like our research group this morning."

"You are so intelligent. How did you know what I was thinking?"

Similar conversations happened after we read Molly Bang's *The Paper Crane* and Gerda Marie Scheidl's *The Crystal Ball*, and after we met the two sisters in John Steptoe's *Mufaro's Beautiful Daughters*. These fictional accounts and folktales had characters or events that were somehow connected to our research studies. It's as if the authors handed us their stories to help children discover the universality of human life. Quality books elevate our daily research. I thank the authors of picture books for enriching our lives by helping us see universality and stretch farther around the world.

These picture books were key to the process of connecting the information and concepts we had learned to other things. Once the children started connecting their research to the characters or events in picture books, they started seeing connections everywhere. Lynn Cherry's *A River Ran Wild* reminded them of our research about recycling and of Martin Luther King, Jr., who worked to make a better world. Emily Arnold McCully's historical fiction, *The Bobbin Girl*—wasn't that just like what Ed Vargas, from the garment workers' union, told us? Vera B. Williams portrays human kindness so simply and colorfully in *Music, Music for Everyone*. Wasn't Rosa kind of like Becky Berman, who helps children in

Guatemala? Ezra Jack Keats' version of *John Henry* reminded us of the work of coal miners as it carried us into the drama of John Henry's heroic life.

In our research groups and classroom life, our language is ordinary. But quality picture books have language that is beautiful, powerful, humorous, and sensitive, and they have different and even extraordinary ways of saying things. They may zoom in on a small incident, an ordinary person, or a single event. They elevate our language and expand our thoughts and vocabularies.

Sometimes I stop after reading a sentence or paragraph and say, "Oh, I have to read that again. Listen." I reread slowly so the music of the words can fill the air. Rereading this way helps the flow and beauty of the language find its way into our hearts and minds, and even into the children's writing. After rereading, I will say something like, "Remember this beautiful language during Writing Workshop." Some children simply enjoy the language, while others work on the flow and quality of their writing.

We sometimes reread when we share the children's writing from Writing Workshop, too. I say, "Will you let me reread that page from your writing? I absolutely love the language." Or, "The way you wrote that reminds me of the way Vera B. Williams said that in . . . which book was that in?" There's always someone who can remind me. Or, "That reminds me of what happened at our interview of . . . ," or "of what we did in research group." And a child will respond, "Oh, yeah, I think so, too."

Literature plays an important role in an inquiry classroom by

- helping children see the relationships between their inquiry and fictional or real characters in literature
- strengthening concepts from our inquiry study
- taking children and adults further from home than they could have imagined
- helping children see new perspectives and have new insights
- helping children meet people of other races and nationalities
- enriching our language through vocabulary and ways of expressing concepts
- exposing children to quality written language—book language
- influencing the quality of the children's writing
- promoting literature children can select during independent reading
- allowing fantasy and imagination into our lives
- bringing joy to our lives

What Kinds of Literature Can We Use?

It's the quality and variety of literature that expands our horizons, so in our inquiry classroom we use many genres of literature.

Poetry. Every day, we begin our afternoon Meeting with poetry. Sometimes a poem is perfect to raise the level of thinking about a particular issue or topic. I have introduced poems at Research Workshop, Reading Workshop, Meeting, and other times of day. I'm always trying to improve our collection of poetry so that it will include

- poems about different topics or issues
- poems by poets of different races, ages, genders, and nationalities
- poems of different styles and types—with or without rhymes; haiku; long, short, and medium-length poems

When we do a formal poetry study for several weeks during Writing Workshop, we always begin by reciting several poems we know by heart. This lets us feel the rhythms and music of the poems and gives us topics for the children's writing. Using several poems lets us experience different styles of writing. Then when the children write, and what we've recited often influences their writing.

You'll often hear Langston Hughes' voice in children's writing, or feel the surprises of Marilyn Singer's nature poems from *Turtle in July*. You can feel the swerving of Monica Gunning's "Jamaican Market Bus" from *Not a Copper Penny in Me House*, or hear a new version of "Snail Race," about a teacher in Trinidad, from *Coconut Kind of Day* by Lynn Joseph.

The poems we write about our research studies become the ones we love to recite at Meeting, celebrations, or random times during the day.

Fiction. In the early part of the year most of the stories we use are picture books. Some children's authors write historical fiction for young children. Later in the year we read some chapter books together.

Nonfiction. Nonfiction is more useful in the Research Workshop than at Meeting. Children seem to prefer the flow of fiction at story time. An occasional nonfiction book finds its way into our Meeting. Books that do are ones where the author has consciously worked on the quality of the language. Lynn Cherry's nonfiction books, for example, sound like poetry and work well at Meeting.

The homemade books that we create after interviews and trips are our own nonfiction literature.

In *Lifetime Guarantees: Toward Ambitious Literacy Teaching* (2000), Shelley Harwayne writes about our school's nonfiction research room, which is filled with print and non-print resources about science, social studies, and other topics. We have since lost the space for this glorious room, but the books were moved to other common areas of the school. If your school doesn't have room for a library, perhaps the families can help create a nonfiction research area.

Lyrics for Songs and Games. A section of our classroom library has songbooks and books of games, including hand-clapping games. We also have books in which one song has been made into a picture book. For example, we have *This Land Is Your Land* and *Mail Myself to You*, both books based on Woody Guthrie songs.

Books by Famous First-Grade Authors. We have a box called "Books by Famous First-Grade Authors." These are books written by the children during Writing Workshop. Their covers are made from wallpaper samples. Children can use these books for pleasure or for reference.

Plays. One of my favorite tools for helping children work on their reading are our homemade plays. We create the scripts together after doing research, then I type the scripts and print copies for the children. The children keep their copies at home so they can practice for a production, and they read and reread the scripts and practice the plays with their friends and families. The scripts help children learn high-frequency and other words and give the children a closer look at punctuation.

Scripts are particularly useful for struggling readers because the children hear and learn the words at rehearsals. Then when they read, they can match the spoken and written words. Sometimes the children are surprised to see what a word looks like in print. I often see a big leap forward in reading during the weeks we practice a play.

Reference Books. Our classroom has several types of reference books:

- children's dictionaries and atlases
- an adult dictionary and atlas
- dictionaries in a few different languages
- science and social studies guidebooks about trees, houses, different countries, and other subjects
- photography books
- art books

How Do We Know Which Book Will Fit?

- Talk to colleagues from your school or other schools.
- Go to a public library and ask the librarian.
- Take courses in children's literature.
- Read publications for educators, such as

  The New Advocate
  Horn Book
  Language Arts
  The children's section of the *New York Times Book Review*
  Educators for Social Responsibility Newsletter
  Rethinking Schools Newsletter
  Teaching for Change: Multicultural Educational Resources

- Look in catalogs of the publishers you respect.
- Read reviews from book clubs such as Scholastic and Trumpet.
- Speak with families.
- Go to a bookstore, particularly one that specializes in children's literature, and ask the workers for suggestions. Eavesdrop on the conversations of other teachers, or politely ask to join them.
- Check on the Internet.

Where Can a Teacher Find Literature?

- Go through your classroom library. I do this before every new inquiry study. Books that you never thought would be useful can suddenly become very helpful.
- Borrow books from colleagues and friends.
- Go to the public library or school library.
- Go to used-book sales at libraries and to tag and garage sales.
- Write to publishers.
- Make a list of the books you want, then ask your principal, PTA, a foundation, or an organization to provide funds for you to purchase the books.
- Find bookstores that sell used books.

Bringing Quality Literature into the Children's Homes

How can we share quality literature with children's families? If children hear quality literature in school, they'll talk about it at home—sometimes. My sons never told me about stories from school. We need ways to make families aware of the literature we're reading and to help them bring literature into their homes. Here are some of the ways I use:

- I write about the books in the *Family Homework*. I sometimes give details to explain how we used a book or what the book is about. I encourage the family to discuss the book.
- In the Family Homework or personal conversations, I encourage families to use the public library and bookstores.
- I let children check books out of the classroom library and take them home.
- I encourage families to purchase books at our two book fairs and street fair. I make sure that families that can't afford to buy books get them anyway. Other families or I contribute money to help.
- I encourage families to exchange books or give books they no longer want to other families.
- I talk with the families about the literature in schoolyard or classroom conversations.

- Our former principal, Shelley Harwayne, organized book clubs for the families.

Reading in an Inquiry Classroom

In our inquiry classroom, the content drives the teaching of skills. We want the children to look and wonder and to ask themselves what a piece of writing will be about. Having some idea of what the writing will be about helps a child figure out new words. We teach children strategies that include phonics, learning high-frequency words, looking for patterns, finding familiar words within bigger words, breaking words into syllables, and using pictures. But knowing the context makes using these strategies easier. If a child knows that a book is about vehicles, she can anticipate that she will find words such as *trucks, cars, helicopters,* or *travel.* When she encounters those words in the book, she can use a combination of her awareness of the topic, the pictures, and her awareness of phonics and sight words to help figure out the words.

Our classroom has an integrated curriculum. Social studies, writing, reading, math, and other subjects are part of the whole picture. Some of the reading is focused on the research studies but many of the books we select aren't. These include collections of text sets and trade books for beginning and more advanced readers. We also have shelves of fiction, ABC books, science books, and poetry. Through our immersion in this rich array of literature, fiction and nonfiction, we teach children to apply these combined strategies. From homemade books about interviews so familiar to them to books with less familiar topics, they learn to look at the context and use those combined strategies.

When Do We Read?

We have Reading Workshop every morning. Two days a week we do word study using our homemade books, a form of guided reading with the whole class. Three days a week small groups of children read independently or with adults. We also read during Research Workshop and at other times of the day.

Children who struggle with reading get extra help through various school programs, including a one-on-one Reading Recovery program and a pullout program where children work in small groups. Family members often come to class to read with one or two children at a time. Senior citizens come to read with the children every week.

Guided Reading

As I select materials for guided reading with the whole class, I look for things that will help me teach specific reading skills while they deepen our understandings from a research study. If we are doing research about athletes, we can read about athletes in poems, song lyrics, fiction and nonfiction books, our own homemade books, the signs and labels on our murals and walls, and on the Internet.

When we read *Wilma Unlimited: How Wilma Rudolph Became the World's Fastest Woman* as part of a research study, we saw the words *black* and *track*. What a perfect opportunity to take a closer look at words with the *ack* ending. We generated a great list of words: *sack, tack, pack, lack, jack, Jack, Mack*. In the process we found words that sound like *ack* words but aren't: *tic tac, McDonald's, macaroni*. This led to conjecture about why those words don't have the *ack* spelling. We laughed about how the English language doesn't always follow the rules. We looked at more *ack* words in the song Ruby's parents wrote about for us about Jackie Robinson. Children saw *ack* words in the books they read during independent reading or at home.

Learning from research study resurfaces in the Reading Workshop and the Family Homework. The *ack* words we studied became part of the next Family Homework, and I explained to the families the context of the *ack* reading assignment, in which the children look for *ack* words in a poem and write sentences for *ack* words or draw pictures of *ack* words.

How Do We Use Poetry for Guided Reading? I often copy a poem onto a chart tablet or overhead projector transparency. During a research study of the Caribbean Islands and South America, I put Monica Gunning's poem "Roadside Peddlers" on a chart tablet. In the poem, you can hear the peddlers calling out to people to buy their fresh fish, mangoes, and tangerines. Their words are in quotation marks. As we read and recited the poem, we raised our voices to get the attention of passersby. What a pleasant way to learn about quotation marks! This poem and another with quotation marks ended up in the Family Homework the next week.

How Do We Use Signs, Labels, and Murals for Guided Reading? Signs, labels, and murals are standard fare in Reading Workshop and at other times during the day. A mural is never finished because children can add details or labels at any time during the year. Signs and labels can have a great value in an inquiry classroom. They document the inquiry and inform our visitors, who may then engage in conversation with the class. Every conversation about a mural serves as a review. Sometimes visitors even add new information or concepts.

If you read and reread a sign or label before it is put up on a mural or poster,

- children will have been introduced to new words.
- children will be conscious of the words and where they are located in the room.
- children can return to the words for help while reading or writing. They can use the words in signs, labels, and murals in the same way we use a word wall.

How Do We Use Our Homemade Books for Guided Reading? Homemade books are set in the context of our research study. The children write these books about an interview or trip. Our homemade books serve several purposes, providing

- a range of possibilities for guided and independent reading.
- an opportunity to review the concepts from an interview or trip.
- a way for children to practice by rereading at home with an adult.
- an opportunity for children not only to review the concepts and information from an interview or trip but also to add a new dimension to work by getting new input, ideas, and perspectives from family members.

We typically begin our guided reading of the homemade books by having a child ask, "What do you predict will be in this book?" When a child predicts a word, I must quickly decide what to do with that word: Record it neatly on our board and have the children copy it in their reading journal? Use it for word study?

We can use our homemade book about Ed Vargas as an example. Ed is a parent from MNS and an organizer at UNITE (Union of Needletrades Industrial and Textile Employees), the garment workers union. A child predicted we would find the word *worker* in the book. I decided to use that word for word study.

"Why would we find the word *worker* in this book about Ed?" I asked.
"Because he helps *workers* who make clothes," the child answered.
"Great," I said.
A child waved her hand. "I see the word *work* in *worker*."
"What a terrific observation!" I responded.

I started to make a word web:

"What did the *workers* do at the factory in El Salvador?" I asked.
"They *worked*," several children responded. We added *worked* to our web.
"What other words with the word *work* or *worker* might be in our book?" I asked.

I added their suggestions to the web:

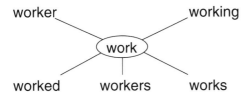

I then suggested the words *workable* and *rework*. We went from one word, *worker*, to eight new words—and we had fun doing it. Later in the day I showed the children where we would post the word web so they could refer to it again.

The children also predicted we'd find the word *factory*. As we sounded it out, we said the sound *e* at the end, but I wrote the letter *y*. "That's strange, I wonder why we put a *y* instead of an *e*," I said. We thought of a bunch of other words that have a *y* at the end: *baby*, *candy*, *funny*, *money*, *try*, *sky*, *silly*, *bunny*, *by*, *my*, *cry*, *family*. Someone noticed that sometimes *y* says *e* and sometimes it says *i*, and we went on to figure out when.

After a delightful discussion, we opened up our book about Ed and circled all of the words that ended with *y*. It was like a treasure hunt. "Oh, I found the word *factory*." "I found the word *by*." "Look, I found *money*." That led to a yearlong exploration for words that end with *y*.

A homemade book may have words that are useful for teaching about these things:

- compound words
- contractions
- consonants or vowels and other elements of phonics
- high-frequency words
- homonyms or homophones
- synonyms or antonyms
- words from other languages
- interesting spellings of words
- punctuation

Homemade books have a limited vocabulary and much repetition. We keep pages that are about the same topic together. In our book about Alicia Perez, from the United Farm Workers, the pages about Alicia picking peaches as a six-year-old were all together. Those five pages had the words *ladder*, *peaches*, *sister*, *brother*, and *boxes*. The seven pages about Alicia helping strawberry workers in California had the words *workers*, *strawberry*, *pesticides*, *pay*, and *boss*. There was so much repetition, the children were bound to absorb those words.

Homemade books lend themselves to working on specific strategies. We add new strategies to our repertoire throughout the year. Strategies include

- looking at the picture to help you figure out a new word
- sounding out or "stretching" out a word
- saying "MMMMMMMM" and reading to the end of the sentence, then guessing the word, checking your guess, and rereading the sentence
- breaking the word into parts or syllables

- thinking about where you saw a word before
- using patterns to help figure out a new word
- using rhymes to help figure out a word

Homemade books are useful because the children know the context, so checking to see if a word makes sense after using these strategies is easier. It's also easy to use discussions about the content to assess children's comprehension skills. Homemade books are particularly useful for second-language learners.

How Do I Know Which Skills or Strategies to Teach from a Particular Homemade Book? As with any book or text set, we must read homemade books before we use them to teach reading. Because I have prepared our homemade books for publication, I know which words a book contains and I have already thought of the words and skills I want to use the book to work on. I usually continue this planning with my student teachers. We sit together with copies of the book and jot down the skills we could teach using that book. Then we discuss our ideas. We wait for the children to make their predictions before we add words or concepts we want to introduce.

After our word study, the children read the homemade books with a partner. We review the strategies we will use when we find "toughie" words. Sometimes I role-play reading with a partner. I act like a terrible partner, looking the other way, humming, and being of no use. The children laugh and joke, and we talk about how to be a good partner:

- Hold the book between you.
- Focus on the book.
- Listen to your partner.
- If your partner has a problem with a word, don't tell him the word, but help him figure it out.
- Take turns.
- Discuss what you or your partner have read.
- Keep your discussion focused on the topic.

As the children read with partners, the adults work with children who need extra help or circulate around the class and listen to the children read. After the second day of word study, children take the homemade books home to read to their families.

Can Homemade Books Be Used with Other Age Groups? Younger children can make different types of homemade books that can be used for informal reading:

- Each child can make a page to include in a big book. Children can write with approximated spelling and the adults will translate it into standard

English using very large print. For children who are not writing yet, adults can take dictation, using very large print. The individual pages can be glued or stapled together into a big book.

- Each child can make a page for a small book using approximated spelling (and translation) or dictation. Copies can be made for the whole class.

With older children there are even more possibilities:

- The children can type, revise, and edit their pages on the computer.
- Small groups of children can write about different interviews or trips. They can work together to edit, revise, and publish their work in a variety of formats.
- Children can create big books to share with story partners in other classes.
- Family members can work with children to revise and edit their books for publication.
- The homemade books will be part of the classroom collection. Rather than having a copy for each child, there can be six or seven in a text set.
- The homemade books can be part of a classroom or school lending library.

How Can We Get Multiple Copies of the Homemade Books? In the survey I take the first week of school, I ask which families have access to a copier at home or at work. If a few do, they take turns printing copies. If no families can print for us, we print our copies at school. Sometimes families donate paper for this.

Summary

In the Appendix there are several excerpts from Family Homework that inform families about the literature we read and the concepts we have dealt with during Reading Workshops. (September 15, October 5, 19, November 2, December 7, January 11, March 8, 22, and April 26.)

Research studies are a wonderful vehicle for developing the love of poetry and other literature and for learning to read. As young children learn to read, they have greater access to resources for their research studies. Literature enhances the quality of inquiry. I hope that my students will continue to seek connections in literature as they search for answers, for literature can bring greater understanding and joy to our lives.

7

Research Study: People Who Make or Drive Vehicles

Who makes or drives bulldozers, cars, trucks, buses, trains, subway trains, planes, motorcycles, helicopters, and bicycles? This topic is certainly not in the New York City Board of Education's first-grade social studies curriculum guide. How did the children come up with such a topic?

September 9 was the first day of school. I invited the families to walk up to our fourth-floor classroom with us. After songs and introductions, I told them about our study of *people at work* and invited their participation. I told them I thought of them as my coworkers.

After the families left, we took a short break and then gathered again on the carpet. I told the children that this year we would be doing research about the jobs people do. I asked, "What jobs would you like to learn about? What would be special for you?"

There were lots of proposals including dancers, athletes, and artists. Some children wanted to know how cars are made. Some wanted to know how trucks are made. The list kept growing as the children added motorcycles, planes, helicopters, and bikes. I asked, "What is the word that describes all of these ways of traveling? After a few suggestions, we settled on the word *vehicle*.

Planning

My student teachers, Pam Wen and Amber Frantz, wanted to work with the groups that were doing research about dance and sports. I had never done an in-depth study about people who make or drive vehicles, so I wasn't ready to start the next day. Besides, I needed more time to help my student teachers plan and gather resources. I suggested to the children that we work on a week-long study of the people who work at our school while we prepared for the vehicle study. We walked through the building and met various staff members and we interviewed a school aide, Dora Cruz.

All that week and the next weekend, I thought about a vehicle study.

- What could we do that would be really interesting?
- Who did I know that we could interview?
- Did I know any poems or stories about the topic?
- I'm not terribly interested in cars, but I'm fascinated with trucks and trains. Where are they going? What are they delivering?
- About subways, Chelsea's father, Stephan, drives the L train.

I asked myself questions.

- Was a study of people who make or drive vehicles big enough?
- Could this sustain us over time?
- Would it interest the children who had chosen to be in the group?
- Was it appropriate for first grade?
- Could we make the learning fun?
- Were there enough age-appropriate resources on the topic or would we have to adapt resources?
- What activities could we do to make it a truly deep learning experience?
- Were there any related trips we could take?

I sat down that weekend and jotted some of my questions about vehicles down in my journal:

Who makes our vehicles?
What are some of the different jobs involved?
What are cars made from?
Who makes those materials?
Where are the materials from?
How are they produced?
Are they from the earth or artificial? (steel, glass, plastic, rubber, etc.)

The next two questions are always in my mind and on my list of considerations:

How can I make this study multicultural in essence?
How can I raise gender issues?

I jotted down possible resources and things we could do:

- Take a trip to a car factory or auto repair shop.
- Watch videos of factories where cars or trucks are produced.

- Contact the United Auto Workers Union and the Transit Workers Union.
- Interview an autoworker, an auto mechanic, or a transit worker.
- Read books and magazines.
- Interview Chelsea's father, Stephan, and ride on his train.
- Visit the bus depot where Dylan's grandfather, Lem, worked before he retired. (Dylan Gibbs was in last year's class.)
- Take trips on buses.
- Make a mural about the people who drive vehicles or about the production of vehicles.

The topic sounded gigantic—there were so many directions we could go in. These were just *my* ideas—just wait until the children and families told me about *their* interests! They might be so different from mine. Our research could go on for months or even the whole school year. I was so excited.

Family Involvement

Thinking about my life experiences, I could see that I had a lot to draw on for this study. The class families, my colleagues, and our friends would give us plenty of resources.

Our Family Homework was the major vehicle for communicating each week with the families. We also had meetings and less formal communication in the schoolyard, in the hall, in the classroom, and on the telephone.

The Family Homework for the week of September 15 included information about our week-long study of the workers in our school. I included some of the math and reading in excerpts so you can see that, wherever possible, I brought in the overall theme of People at Work. You will also see the informal tone of the communication with the families.

The Appendix has excerpts of the Family Homework that covered this research study on September 15, October 5, and 19, November 2, December 7, January 11, February 1, March 8, and other dates.

Who Was in Our Research Group?

Because I had student teachers, we were able to form small research groups. However, this inquiry study could have been done by the whole class. All of the interviews and trips involved the whole class. The research groups included six boys and girls representing a wide range of life experiences and academic skills. Some of these children were already reading and some hardly knew letters or sounds. That was just fine. Aneta and Romina had only a mild interest in the topic at first.

Samuel, Ian-Michael, Tamiko, and Jordan Nassau were fascinated by cars and trucks, construction vehicles, and motorcycles.

Interest in the topic is the main factor that attracts children to a research group, but sometimes children join a group just to be with a friend, a particular student teacher, or with me.

All the children would bring their life experiences into the research group. Aneta had traveled a lot by plane to the Czech Republic, where she was born, while Ian-Michael had flown to visit relatives in Hong Kong. Tamiko loved bikes, motorcycles, and cars that were popular with his big brother. All the children had traveled by cars, taxis, buses, and subways.

Research Workshop: The Three Steps for Beginning the Research (Days 1–2, with Paula)

We started with the three essential steps for beginning any research project:

- finding out what prior knowledge of the topic we have
- giving the children an opportunity to ask questions or tell their interests
- having the children think of ways to find information about the topic

Tapping into Prior Knowledge

"What do you know about vehicles?" I asked. The children talked with great enthusiasm about their bicycles, skates, and skateboards. We heard stories of car trips some had taken. Everyone had been on buses and subways. Some had been on long-distance trains. Some were fascinated by construction vehicles. The children had a lot of prior knowledge about types of vehicles and some information about people who drive vehicles, but little information about people who make vehicles. Knowing what the children knew would inform my teaching.

Asking Questions

The children's questions, my questions, and family members' questions would be the focus of our research study. I asked, "What would you like to know about people who make cars and trucks and trains and other vehicles?" I wrote the children's questions down on a chart tablet so we could refer back to them.

Our Questions About the People Who Make Vehicles
Who makes them?
How do they learn to make them?
How do they make them?
What are the cars and trucks made from?

Where do they make them?
How do people learn to drive them?
What happens at a car wash?

If your students have had little experience asking questions in school, they may need some help to formulate questions. I told the children some things that really fascinate me about trucks or trains so they could hear not only my questions themselves, but also different ways of asking questions. I asked things like "I wonder where they get the rubber to make the tires?" "Gee, I really want to know who makes the subway trains." "How do you learn to drive a subway train? Is it hard to do?" The teacher's questions usually get the children started on asking their own.

Thinking of Ways to Find Answers

To help the children think of ways to find answers, I asked, "How can we get this information?" They responded with these suggestions:

We can look in books.
We can ask people.

This was our first research study, so the suggestions were limited. I wrote them on a chart. It would be my responsibility to help the children find additional tools for the research. Before long, they would have a long list of ways to get information.

Share Time

At Share Time the children shared their list of questions with the rest of class.

Reflecting on the Teaching

What Can You Do When You Don't Have Enough Resources? Living in a big city, I knew that the children had seen or been in many types of vehicles. Doing research about people who drive vehicles for a living could be interesting, but I didn't think I could get enough resources for early readers to sustain the research on a day-to-day basis. Perhaps we could do the research about people who drive or operate vehicles at the same time we researched people who make vehicles.

Expanding the Research Outside of the Classroom: A Trip

To whet their appetites, I took the whole class for a walk down the street from our school, as I would on many other occasions. There was a large delivery truck in front of the school. I asked the workers if they would take a few moments to say hello and answer our questions. Most workers are happy to stop for a short time to answer schoolchildren's questions.

So right away we were out and about asking questions and hearing each other ask questions. Asking focused questions is a skill. I wanted our questions to focus on job-related issues, so in the beginning of the year I modeled asking job-related questions. After the workers had agreed to answer questions, I asked, "What are you delivering to our school?" Then I asked the children to ask the workers about their job. The children asked,

What is your job?
What time do you start in the morning?
How long do you work?
How did you learn to drive that big truck?

Ordinarily, I would stop to let the children take notes. But these workers were on the move and we didn't want to take too much of their time. So after our thank-yous, I told the children to take notes in their research journals. I told them they could draw pictures, use words, or both. It was the beginning of the school year, so most of the notes were made with pictures.

We continued down the block and stopped to look at parked cars and at the cars and trucks going past. At the corner was a construction site. My previous class had the pleasure of watching the huge bulldozers, backhoes, and other equipment at this site. Now we saw a big crane, trucks delivering building supplies, and lots of cement trucks. After several more walks to the site, I realized that it wouldn't be the ideal spot to observe for our vehicle research. It was fine for an occasional visit to identify vehicles, meet the workers, and observe the progress, but there wasn't enough there to sustain us at this stage of the construction.

I hoped that stopping for informal interviews with truck drivers and other vehicle operators would start the children on a lifelong habit of observing workers and asking them questions (with an adult present, and later on their own).

Family Involvement

In the Family Homework, I wrote, "We have learned so much just by taking time to speak to people at the construction site." I wanted the families to see our strategies for doing research. Stopping to ask questions is an important way to learn. I hoped families would do the same thing with their children when they were out walking or traveling. I also wanted family members to know that there are many different ways to participate in their children's learning. Not every family member can come into the classroom or go on trips with us, and that's just fine. I present many other ways to participate in the Family Homework. I want families to know that I appreciate them participating in any of these ways.

Planning

Teaching a Mandated Topic

Soon after the research group got started, our new student teacher, Karen Dunlap, arrived from the Midwest for a short placement. I asked her to take over my research group. I wanted her to go through the same thinking process that I had gone through several weeks before.

Karen was really scared because this was definitely not her area of strength. I urged her to imagine that she was assigned to a class in any school. All of us are required to teach about topics we may not love or think we are prepared to teach. If we have little prior knowledge about the production of vehicles or any other topic, we must become researchers.

Despite her fears, Karen took the challenge. She explored Internet sites and used her local public library to find piles of books about car production. She started talking about the topic with local friends and e-mailed her friends back home in Indiana, a car-producing region.

We had many discussions during school and on our rides home together. I asked Karen about her prior knowledge of the topic. I told her about the children's initial questions and interests and asked her to think about these issues: This topic is part of a yearlong study of People at Work. The children want to know about the production of vehicles—that was their first question. There is much to know about car production. I asked Karen

- What do you want to know about car production; what interests you?
- Since these are young children, and there are endless things to learn about car production, what do you think are important facts or issues for first graders?
- Which of these topics is feasible to work on with young children?

We didn't need to worry about time because I could resume working with the group after Karen left.

It would have been much easier for me to hand Karen a curriculum guide about car production. There's comfort in having things spelled out for you. You don't get that terrible feeling of inadequacy that comes from not being sure what lies ahead. There is no curriculum guide about vehicle production for early childhood or elementary school. Most young children are not engaged in formal research studies at all, so there aren't curriculum guides for most research studies.

Most of the books and Internet sites about vehicle production are for older children and adults. This places an added responsibility on teachers. We have to become researchers ourselves and reach out for information everywhere we can.

We have to learn to make the materials at hand useful for young people by doing things like reading a segment from a book and turning the information into a role-play to make it accessible to the children.

The topic was enormous. Karen needed to find a hook, a way into the research. After quite of bit of exploration and discussion, we found something quite practical—the assembly line.

Research Workshop: The Assembly Line or Production Line (Days 3–7, with Karen)

To address the children's question "How are cars made?" Karen pulled out our Lego collection and sorted the pieces to use in simulating an assembly line. The next morning, the children used Legos to design a simple car-like object. Karen then had the children line up on either side of a cabinet that was covered with a sheet of oilcloth. Each child was in charge of one type of Lego—one car part—and represented one worker at the automobile factory. Karen pulled the oilcloth—the conveyor belt—along as the workers constructed a car on the assembly line.

Oh, that was fun. The children wanted to do it again. That was great—it's important for them to repeat processes. As they worked, there was a lot to talk about:

- the vocabulary of assembly-line work
- the importance of working together
- the repetitive nature of the job
- related problems for the workers

The children looked at photographs of assembly lines. Karen wrote some of the important vocabulary—the key words—on a the board: *assembly line, production line, conveyor belt, worker,* and so on—not your typical first-grade vocabulary. After the children drew pictures of the assembly line in their research journals, Karen told them to copy the key words and make labels on their pictures. Later we added the words to our classroom Word Wall as the whole class watched so that they too would be able to use them.

The group went back to the assembly line for several days of Research Workshop. At first, this seemed repetitive to Karen. But each time the children went back, they both reviewed and gathered new information. In the process of producing cars, they had had to

- plan
- work together cooperatively
- keep on working because the assembly line was still moving

- stay focused
- marvel at the Lego car they had produced

Share Time

The children showed the class their assembly line. Everyone was so excited. Ben asked, "Isn't that like at the airport?" I showed my delight: "What a fantastic observation, Ben. You are amazing." My enthusiasm was deliberate: I knew it would stimulate more thinking. Immediately Ashley said, "That's like at the supermarket."

Children thought about escalators and other places with conveyor belts. This hooked the whole class into the vehicle research. Everyone wanted to make cars at the assembly line and at Center Time that week several children tried it.

Reflecting on the Teaching

Finding Connections. The discussions during Share Time often led to deeper thinking as children made connections. Ben's comment about the assembly line helped us find a hidden treasure of relationships: the assembly line is like the conveyor belt at the supermarket; people work together to build cars or houses. After a while, the children were able to find connections without the help of a teacher.

The children soon saw that some of the other research groups dealt with the same issues they did. The concepts of people cooperating, focusing, and working hard or practicing repeatedly were the very ones that Pam's dance research group was struggling with while learning a Chinese dance.

Sometimes recognition of common issues came from the children during Share Time: "We talked about that in our group, too." Sometimes I pointed connections out: "Wow, what Karen's group did at the assembly line sounds a lot like what Pam's group said the other day. What do you think I mean by that?"

We found more and more connections. A child from Amber's sports research group said, "Sammy Sosa and Mark McGwire had to practice and stay focused, too." Later in the year the same issues came up during our interviews of Jodi Schulson, a builder, and Jennifer Crowl, a Rockette. It is our responsibility as teachers to help children find common threads in our research.

Family Involvement

I knew that if we told the families about the assembly line and about the concept of division of labor that we were working on, they would add their own life experiences and knowledge. This happened in many homes. Discussions took place at the supermarket and families made discoveries as they were out walking, shopping, watching TV, and so on.

Research Workshop: Making a Movie (Days 8–11, with Karen)

After several days of work, Karen helped the children make a movie about their assembly line (not quite as good as Charlie Chaplin's movie, *Modern Times*, but a good first-grade movie). Here's how they did it:

- First, the group talked about the movie and what they wanted to show.
- Then they used crayons and markers on strips of cash register paper to draw the workers on the assembly line. One child had a habit of drawing pretty rainbows on all of her pictures, which didn't quite fit with the concept of an assembly line. Karen helped the child revise her movie segment, just as we revise work at Writing Workshop.
- Karen cut rectangular holes at either end of a shoebox. The children threaded the paper movie through the holes in the box. It looked like a TV show.
- After a few days of work, the children tape-recorded the audio for their movie.

Share Time

It's so important that children see themselves as teachers—of their peers and of adults. Sharing their homemade movie with their families and classmates gave the group that opportunity, as the Family Homework of October 19 shows.

Research Workshop: Using the Newspaper (Day 12, with Karen)

Once your class gets involved in a particular research topic, you'll notice relevant information everywhere. I found a newspaper article about some cars that were being recalled. What a perfect teaching opportunity. I suggested that Karen read the article to her group. She did, then they role-played the recall of their Lego cars.

Share Time

I wanted Karen to see how to use Share Time to get the whole class involved in an issue, so that day at Share Time I organized a role-play for the whole class. We pretended that each group of children had a different type of car. I read excerpts from the newspaper article. When I read about a particular car being recalled, the children who had that kind of car had to take it to the service station for repair. They were so disappointed when their cars were recalled. Because I talked about this role-play in the Family Homework, over the course of the year several children brought in articles about other product recalls.

Reflecting on the Teaching

Bringing Current Events into the Research Study. Why interject newspaper articles into ongoing research? Because it helps move the research from theory to real life. Yes, in the real world, something wrong happened in the production of a certain vehicle model. Perhaps the parts were defective, there was a design flaw, or there was a problem on the assembly line. The reality is that people make mistakes that can cause injury or even death. In real life, owners have to bring their cars in for repairs. There are also recalls of tires, car seats, toys, foods, and many other products.

This morning a headline in the *New York Times* caught my attention: "Citing Children, EPA is Limiting Use of a Pesticide" (August 3, 1999). I couldn't resist reading the article. The issue of pesticides had come up during our interview of Alicia Perez of the United Farm Workers and during our work on the play *The Person Behind the Thing.*

As I read, I said to myself, "I wonder how many of the adults from our class will show this article to their children." Later in the day, I thought, "I hope it will be on the radio and TV news. Then maybe some of the children will hear it for themselves." I smiled and thought, "I know some of the children will find out about this. I'm sure they will. This is why I'm teaching."

I want our classroom research to bring lifelong changes to our consciousness—the children, the families, and me. I want to change our reading, radio-listening, and TV-watching habits. When the children hear the words *car* or *car production, assembly* or *production line,* or *recalls,* I want them to think "I remember when we did research about that in first grade," or, "We did that in first grade." When they hear the word *pesticide,* I want it to ring a bell in their minds so they will make a mental note, make their research part of an upcoming conversation, or maybe even participate in some kind of social action.

The recall of cars wasn't one of our original questions about how vehicles are made. In a research study, you can take steps to the side. You can and should bring current events into the research.

Research Workshop: Making a Model Car (Day 13, with Karen and Denise Stabenau)

The children were still addressing how cars are made. One weekend I searched high and low for simple, non-glue car models. Karen and I were uncomfortable directing the model making, so I asked in the Family Homework if any family member could come to work with the research group. We would adjust to the time that was best for them.

Annelise's mother, Denise, joined the group during Research Workshop and worked with the children to produce a lovely, shiny car. They had a chance to see some of the many parts that go into a car.

Share Time

When the children in the research group shared the car they had made, other children couldn't wait to make a car. We had a second model car ready for them at Center Time. We talked as we worked. During the discussion, I asked the children to think about how so many parts are used for just one car (and this was a simple model). I asked them to think about where the parts came from and who made them.

Family Involvement

Curriculum Night. This is a schoolwide activity in late October. Family members who didn't get to come to our classroom often saw a big change from the first day of school. The room was now filled with murals, photographs, pictures, dioramas, posters, and signs. The Word Wall was filling up with a delightful combination of high-frequency words and words from our research. All these things were documentation of our research. The room was filled with the spirit of our research studies.

I took a lot of time to explain our research to the families, describing how we ask questions about a topic or issue and search for ways to find answers. I talked about the importance of our daily Share Time. I told them that as the year went on, there would be new research topics and their children would have a chance to change topics. Then we had questions and answers and a good discussion.

Interview: Stephan Grant—September 28

Chelsea's father was a train operator for the Metropolitan Transportation Authority. He drove the L train. Fortunately, Stephan Grant was off on Mondays. He came to class loaded down with tools and his bright fluorescent vest. What a big thrill. Chelsea was so happy and so proud.

Stephan answered the children's many questions. As he showed them his tools, we role-played Stephan's job. Wearing the vest was probably the most fun. We talked about health and safety problems, like the garbage on the tracks that attracts rats. Stephan asked for our help to keep the subway system clean.

Not long ago, Stephan's job title was Motorman. We had a good discussion when Stephan told us that his new title was Train Operator. We tried to figure out why the title had changed. I asked, "I wonder how women got to become subway train operators?" and we discussed that issue on upcoming days. This topic of jobs

Figure 7–1. Chelsea's father, Stephan Grant, Paula, and Elwin Walker with the class at the interview.

that excluded women and minorities came up many more times during the year when we did research about health care workers, dancers, and athletes.

Stephan answered our question about how he learned to do the job. That was one of our original questions from the first week of school. Of course, someone asked, "Can we ride on your train?" Stephan invited us to ride the L train with him.

After the interview, each child wrote a page for our homemade book about Stephan. (See Figure 7–2.) We used that book for Reading Workshop a few weeks later.

Family Involvement

Telling the families about our invitation to ride the L train was essential for two reasons: We needed formal permission and more adults to accompany us. This trip would be rich in content. That's why I put it in the Family Homework for several weeks in October. Several parents brought in subway maps for us to use with a homework assignment.

Extending the Research Outside the School: A Trip

If you've ever waited for a movie star or other celebrity to arrive, you'll know what it was like when Stephan's L train arrived at 14th Street and 8th Avenue, the last stop in Manhattan. Stephan's friends, the other train operators and conductors,

Figure 7–2. Julie Avellino's page from the homemade book *Stephan Is a Train Operator, A Book About Chelsea's Father*. September.

told us that the next train was his, so we were ready. We could see Stephan through the window. There was screaming and shouting and great joy. "Stephan, Stephan!"

You can imagine how Chelsea felt. After many hugs, we boarded the train. Stephan took us under the river and through Brooklyn. When we arrived back in Manhattan, we walked from the train and crowded into Phoebe's apartment, where we ate lunch. Several parents accompanied us on this delightful trip. (See the article in *Instructor* magazine, April 1999).

Planning

The interview with Stephan and the trip were part of our major research study about people who make or drive vehicles. I wondered how we could extend the interview into other curriculum areas. The trick was to get my student teachers to wonder, too. How could the interview become part of a multidisciplinary curriculum? The student teachers and I sat around a table with a multidisciplinary planning chart in front of us. We filled in the chart with suggestions for activities in nearly every curriculum area. There were so many possibilities that we knew we wouldn't be able to do all of them.

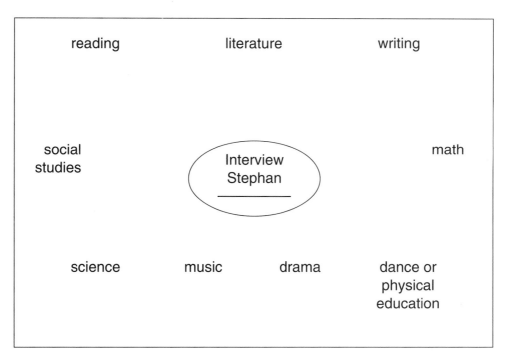

Extending the Research into Reading Workshop

Chelsea beamed on the day we read the homemade book about her father. The children predicted which words they would find in the book: *tools, train, father, subway, garbage, drive, work,* and more. The children copied some of the words from the board into their reading journals. We used other words for word study.

When someone predicted we would see the word *work,* I asked if they needed my help spelling the word. Oh, no, they insisted. That word was all over our room—"People at Work" was on our classroom door and a web of the word *work* hung from a shelf (*work, worker, working, worked, works*). The children were quick to point out other locations of the word.

We made a web for the word *drive: driving, drives, driver.* When I said, "Yesterday Stephan _____ the train," we surprised a few children with the word *drove.* First graders get a kick out of the irregularities of the English language.

Earlier in the year we had talked about words, like *drive*, that lose the *e* when you add *ing*. When I wrote *driving* on the chart tablet, I stopped in the middle to find out how to spell it. The children told me to "throw the *e* out the window!" We hung our new web from a shelf. We returned to it many times during the year.

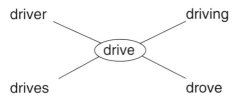

The children put down their journals as we stopped to look at other words that had the same *ai* spelling as *train*. What a long list it was: *rain, main, pain, bait, wait,* etc. When I asked the children to copy five of the words into their reading journals, most rushed to copy all of them. That's a little trick of mine: Whenever I say "copy three" or "copy five" to first graders, a bit of defiance sets in and they must copy more than that. It's funny, and it works. The children will recognize *ai* words, be able to sound out new ones, and use *ai* words in their future writing and reading. This exercise was also fun because it was part of reading the book about Chelsea's father, whom we loved so much.

At the end of our first Reading Workshop with our book about Stephan, the children got to open their own copies of the book and search for the words they had copied into their journals. It was like a treasure hunt, and it gave them a chance to practice

- finding words over and over
- searching from left to right to find the words
- going from top to bottom on the page to find the words
- finding the different forms of words. There were shouts like "I found *driving*." "I found *driver*." "There's the word *drove*."

Also exciting were the shouts of "Look, there's my page!"

Extending the Research into Center Time

Painting a Mural. The next day a group of children chose to paint a mural about our trip to the L train. We gathered at our painting area, made a plan, and then started by making pictures with crayon. Then we put on our smocks (my son's old T-shirts) and set to work painting. We reminisced about the trip. Of course,

Chelsea got to paint her father in the front of the subway train. Later in the week children made labels for the mural and edited them so they would be in standard English. Often that year, children walked over to the mural during Writing Workshop to check on the spelling of key words: *subway, train, train operator,* and *father.*

Extending the Research into Math Workshop

Making Patterns. During our subway trip, we stopped to look at the signs in the subway and at the fantastic patterns in the tiles. Later, while we waited for Stephan, the children initiated looking at the other patterns.

A few days later, Amber, our student teacher, planned a math lesson. She reminded the children how we had looked at the patterns in the tiles. Using the overhead projector and plastic shapes, first Amber, then the children, created their own patterns. Then they used some commercially produced shapes with adhesive on the back to create patterns. Amber attached the children's patterns to our subway mural, which we hung in a prominent location in our room so we could admire it for the rest of the year.

I was really pleased with Amber's lesson. I'm always looking for ways to bring math into a research study, and it's even more important to me that my student teachers do so.

Calculating Numbers. For our math challenge, we pretended we were back in the subway with Stephan. We looked at combinations of numbers totaling ten. The question was, "If you could have only ten people on the subway train, how many men and how many women could you have?"

The children could use cubes or discs, fingers, or mental math to calculate the answer. They worked in pairs. Some groups took the slow route, calculating each time. Others saw the pattern in the numbers and didn't have to do calculations:

men	women	
1 +	_____	= 10
5 +	_____	= 10
7 +	_____	= 10
4 +	_____	= 10
8 +	_____	= 10
9 +	_____	= 10
3 +	_____	= 10
2 +	_____	= 10
6 +	_____	= 10

Interview: Jodi Schulson—October 6

Eliana Slurzberg's mother, Lucy, was anxious for us to interview her friend Jodi Schulson, a home builder who also volunteers to read to children at a hospital. Lucy wanted the children to see this marvelous example of social action. That was important to me, but it wasn't connected to our research topic and I like to keep our work focused. After some thought, I realized that home building has similarities to producing vehicles on an assembly line: There is division of labor. There are people working together.

We decided that we would first interview Jodi about building homes, then talk about her volunteer work.

Jodi came to class with architect's plans and pictures. As she described the many different jobs involved in building a home, we did role-plays. We role-played the people who build the foundation, the people who build the frame, the plumbers, the electricians, and so on. Each part of the job was done by a different subcontractor, represented by a different bunch of children in our role-play.

I asked, "Does this remind you of any other job we've talked about?" The children remarked that it was similar to car production, because each group of people on the assembly line does one particular job. Later in the year, we got to see a real example of division of labor when we visited the Kraft Hat Company in the Bronx as part of our study of garment workers.

After role-playing each type of worker, we stopped to take notes in our interview journals. It was early in the year—October—so the notes were mostly pictures, a few letters, and the key words I had written on the board. We talked about how wonderful it is that Jodi takes time from her busy life to help sick children, and we decided that we would collect some books for her program.

Extending the Research into Reading Workshop

A few weeks after we interviewed Jodi, we used our homemade book for a reading lesson. As we made predictions about what would be in the book, our thoughts turned back to the interview. As part of word study, we made a word web using the word *build*: *build, building, builder, rebuild, builds, built*. The children loved the word *built* because it broke the pattern.

Extending the Research Through Art

The Quilting Bee. Our class created a quilt to reflect our research about people at work. Parents and other family members joined us on several occasions. Each child volunteered to make a patch about someone we interviewed or about a research topic. Children created several patches related to the vehicle research. Chelsea got to make the patch about her father, the L train operator.

Figure 7–3. Chelsea Grant's patch about her father, Stephan. This patch is part of the People at Work quilt.

Planning

Karen and I talked about what direction her research group should take for her remaining weeks in our class. We went back to the children's questions:

Who makes the cars?
What are they made from?
Where do they make the cars?

We thought it might be exciting for the children to look at the things cars are made from and learn who makes those things.

Research Workshop: What are Cars Made From? (Days 14–15, with Karen)

Karen had some really slick advertisements from a car dealership near her apartment. The children in her group looked through the brochures to see what the cars were made from. The main products they identified were metal, rubber, and glass. They turned the pictures into mobiles by cutting the photos, gluing them onto cardboard, attaching them to strings, and attaching the strings to a bent coat hanger. We hung the mobiles for all to see. While the children were at work on the mobiles, they decided their first focus would be on who makes the rubber for cars and how it is made.

Share Time

The children showed the class their car mobiles and talked about their upcoming research on the production of rubber. The class was fascinated by the mobiles.

Extending the Research into Center Time

Making Car Mobiles. The other children wanted to make their own car mobiles, and they did so at Center Time. Within a few days, nearly everyone had added a car to a mobile or had made their own mobile. We hung the mobiles from a rope that went from one side of the room to the other.

Family Involvement

The Family Homework of November 2 informed the families about the interdisciplinary nature of our research study. Some research topics and interviews lend themselves to work in many subject areas. Stephan's interview was one of these. Because I wrote about this in the homework, it became an experience for the whole family.

Research Workshop: Creating a Diorama (Days 16–18, with Karen)

Karen's group looked at books and photographs of people making rubber. They role-played the different jobs, from tapping the trees to getting the rubber to the car factory. After several meetings of Research Workshop, the children in the group constructed a large diorama about rubber production. They used paper towel rolls, construction paper, cardboard, and tempera paints to make trees and scenery, and plasticine to make workers.

Share Time

The whole class loved the diorama. Some offered to help at Center Time. We displayed the diorama in a prominent area so children would stop to look and read the labels.

Research Workshop: Producing a Skit About Rubber Production (Days 19–21, with Karen)

The research group created a short skit to teach the entire class and others about rubber production. The skit helped the children review the sequence of the production process, work together, and enunciate their words. The skit had both choral speaking and individual parts so that everyone would be a full participant.

Share Time

The children practiced their scenes for the class, then proudly presented the skit at the Family Celebration in November. We want children to view sharing information as a form of social action, of informing the community about such an important topic.

Family Involvement

Student teachers are on different kinds of schedules. Some work for six weeks, some for eight, and some even longer, so I just have to be flexible. I was hoping that when Karen left I'd be able to find a family member to take over her group for their study about how steel parts are made, so I advertised our need in the Family Homework.

After Alex's arrival from Bulgaria in October, I had invited his mother, Irena Stefanov, to join us in class. For a few months, Irena helped in the classroom several days a week, also serving as Alex's interpreter as she helped. By November, Irena knew the children pretty well. I learned that Irena had worked in Bulgaria at a company that made steel mills and equipment for steel mills, which it sold around the world. Irena called home to get more information and brochures about her company. She would tell us more about them later in the year.

Irena would have been the perfect person to take over Karen's group, and I asked her if she would. Irena was terrified—she thought she didn't have the right teaching techniques. My goal was to have her continued participation, not to scare her, so I backed off.

The Woody Guthrie research group that I was working with had stopped meeting formally after the November Family Celebration. I just loved the potential in the topic of what vehicles are made from, so I decided that I would return to the research group about people who make or drive vehicles. Irena was happy when I suggested that we work with the group together. She proved to be a far better teacher than she imagined she would.

Research Workshop: Learning About Steel Production (Day 22, with Irena and Paula)

After the November Family Celebration, the children were allowed to change research groups. The new focus of the vehicles group was on the steel used in vehicles.

Tapping into Prior Knowledge

We asked the children what they already knew about steel. They knew it was hard and that sometimes it was shiny. They knew it was used for things like cars, chairs, and train tracks.

Asking Questions

To get the questioning started, I told the children that steel is just like cakes or salads because it's made of many ingredients. The children wanted to know what the ingredients were and where they came from.

Thinking of Ways to Find Answers

Although Irena and I knew many of the answers, we asked the children to think of ways to find answers. They had several months of formal research experience behind them, so they offered several possibilities:

> Read books.
> Read magazines.
> Ask questions of people who know about steel.
> Interview people who make steel.
> Look on the Internet.
> Go to a steel mill.

Share Time

The children in the research group shared their discussion and questions with the rest of the class. We gave all the children time to touch things made from metal in the classroom. Some of the children had prior knowledge to add to our base of information.

Planning

Steel production is a tough topic, and I wondered how first graders could do research about it. I thought hard, and I lost sleep. I talked with friends, family members, and colleagues. I jotted down every possibility on one of my planning sheets. I wondered about reading, writing, literature, art, drama, science, and math—how could we learn about steel through work in those curriculum areas? And where would we find resources?

Irena and I combed through our public libraries and the Internet. Irena even downloaded a video about steel production from the Internet. I found out later in the year that the Library of Congress makes copies of photographs available to students for research.

My friend Robbie Simpson works in the geology department at a local college. I asked her to give or lend us samples of iron ore, coal, and other materials related to steel production, and she did. The children touched, observed, and did role-plays using the samples.

In talking with our student teacher, Pam, I found out that her father was a retired steelworker from Pittsburgh. He sent us samples of the materials used in steel production. We touched and observed the materials at Research Workshop and used them at dramatic play during Center Time.

Research Workshop: Role-Plays About the Ingredients of Steel (Days 23–24, with Irena and Paula)

We started our research by looking in books. The library books we'd found were for middle and high school students, so Irena and I paraphrased the information and looked with the children at the pictures and captions. We looked, read, and talked together.

Irena and I told the children what we already knew about making steel. First, we would focus on coal, which was so important in the production of steel. I had been to an underground coal mine and a strip mine, so I brought in samples of coal and fossils of leaves.

As we gathered information, we role-played the ancient story of how coal is formed and mined. The children played trees that stood tall millions of years ago, then died. (I wondered what a visitor who saw them lying on the classroom floor would say.) We pretended that over the years the trees got covered with layers of mud, rain, and rocks and gradually turned to coal. We stopped the role-play so that the children could draw diagrams with labels in their research journals.

Then the earth rumbled—we created an earthquake to expose some of the coal. That was fun. As we let millions of years flash by, I drew a picture of the vein of coal deep underground. We talked and asked questions, then the children made sketches and labels in their journals.

Next the children role-played miners going deep underground in a locomotive. They took their "pickaxes" and got to work, and I introduced the song "Sixteen Tons." The whole class sang that song and swung their "pickaxes" at Meeting Time the rest of the year. The children begged to repeat the role-play the next day, so we suggested that we build a coal mine in the block area. They jumped at the suggestion.

Share Time

When the group shared the role-play with the rest of the class, all of the children were soon fallen trees covered with mud for millions of years. They loved that.

Extending the Research into Center Time

Working in the Coal Mine. That day at Center Time a group of children started building the coal mine. We covered a table with a large black cloth to represent the coal. My sons' Duplo train tracks and cars wound their way under the table and around the block area. Samples of coal from our rock collection became props. Over time, the children made signs and labels for the coal mine, and the mine evolved as the study evolved.

Family Involvement

When we are making a transition to new research groups or a new topic, I let the families know ahead of time through the Family Homework. This stimulates discussion at home, and it gives us an opportunity to gather resources. Advance notice is an essential part of the planning process, since planning is partly based on available resources, which sometimes come from families. Families provided a number of materials for the coal mine. Notifying the families also helps us gather information.

Research Workshop: Worker Safety (Days 25–26, with Irena and Paula)

We repeated our coal mine role-play for several days by popular demand. I told the children about some issues I thought were relevant, including the methane gas that's produced when trees turn into coal. Sometimes the gas causes terrible explosions. One of our books told about the canaries miners took into coal mines in the old days. If a canary died, the miners knew there was methane gas there and they could rush out of the mine to safety.

The children were sad that the canaries died, but appreciated that their deaths helped save miners. I responded, "That is so sad. What could the miners do so they wouldn't have to use the canaries?" The children suggested that someone could invent a machine to tell the miners when there was methane. In fact, that's what had happened. We looked at pictures of the machine, which led to a discussion about how and why new things are invented. Inventions are often meant to make things easier or safer for people—an important lesson. Amazing topics come up while we search for answers to our questions.

When we interviewed Raymond Oberdecker on December 15, the children asked him about the canaries. Raymond's father had told him about the canaries, too, so we had a real person confirm what we had learned from books. As I sit revising this book, there is a report on the news of a tragic mine explosion in Utah. I wonder how many of my students heard the report and wondered what went wrong.

Share Time

The class was fascinated by the story of the canaries, so we let them do a quick role-play. Then we talked about the invention for sensing methane. Many of the families knew about this invention and discussed it at home even before I wrote about it in the Family Homework the next week. I knew that this Share Time discussion was effective because the children took the initiative to talk about it at home.

Research Workshop: Health and Safety Issues
(Day 27, with Irena and Paula)

Each time we went back to the role-plays, I played the boss and Irena and the children were the workers. The working conditions were awful and I made them worse by not caring about the miners' health and safety. I played the bad guy because I didn't want the children to think of Irena as uncaring. Young children long associate people with the roles they play. My students knew me so well that, no matter what character I role-played, they knew I was just acting.

Another issue I told the children about was the coal dust in the air deep in the mine. They coughed and role-played getting very sick. One of the children remarked, "That's just like in *The Bobbin Girl*." We had read Emily Arnold McCully's book, which is about the mill workers in Lowell, Massachusetts, in 1834, during Meeting Time earlier in the year. The mill workers had contracted brown lung disease from the lint in the air.

"So," I asked, "what would we call it when the coal dust gets into the miners' lungs and makes it difficult to breathe?" "Black lung disease," they guessed. "What could the miners do about that?" I asked. The children had lots of very good suggestions, some of which, I pointed out, were exactly what had happened.

Role-playing again, I was the mean boss who didn't care about the miners' health and refused to make any changes. The children were angry. "Well, what could you do about this?" I asked. "I'm not changing."

We had already talked about unions in our research groups and at earlier interviews. The children talked about strikes and other actions and we role-played some of their proposals, including passing a law to protect the miners. Later, when we interviewed Brenda Davis and Phil Batton, both confirmed that things we had role-played had actually happened. Much later in the year, Ed Vargas, a union organizer and parent from Manhattan New School, told us even more.

Share Time

We did a shortened version of one of the role-plays for the whole class.

Research Workshop: Role-Playing the Production of Coke
(Day 28, with Irena and Paula)

We went back to our reference books, looking at pictures and captions and reading some of the text. A few of the children read to the group. We then did role-plays, including one where some of the coal was taken to a special oven where it was changed to coke, the actual ingredient used in steel production. The children carried small signs to show which ingredient they represented. They insisted on doing the role-play over and over again, and we talked and took notes.

Share Time

We did a shortened version of the role-play for the class.

Research Workshop: The Role of Workers in Steel Production
(Days 29–30, with Irena and Paula)

On the day we role-played making the steel, each child held a sign with the name of an ingredient. With all of the ingredients ready to put in the blast oven, I stopped talking. The children looked around to see what had happened, then asked why I had stopped the role-play—what was wrong. I was silent at first, then I teased, "Something is missing. We have all the ingredients we should put into the blast oven, but nothing is happening. What's missing? Why can't we get the blast oven to work?"

It took a while before the children realized that no one had been given the part of a steelworker! They rolled on the floor with laughter. Some of the children gave up their signs saying "iron ore" and made new ones saying "worker." The workers then made sure the ingredients were put into the oven and took care of the other jobs. The next day, they pleaded with me to do the role-play again.

Figure 7–4. Paula and her research group role-play how steel is made. Samuel Herscher, who is wearing a hard hat, is one of the workers. Dylan Levitt is the oxygen. Ali Greenberg and Jordan Nassau, who are on the floor, are the steel. Eliana Slurzberg is the fire.

Share Time

The children reported about our role-play to the class. Of course, everyone wanted to do that role-play. It was critical that the whole class understand the importance of the workers, so, we did an abbreviated version of the role-play.

Research Workshop: Cooking our Own "Steel" (Day 31, with Irena and Paula)

I kept wondering how we would take the process of making steel from abstraction and theory to reality without going to a steel mill. A mill is no place for young children to visit. Irena and I kept reading to try to understand the process better. When we read the word *mold*, I thought of Jell-O molds. Ah, there it was—we would make Jell-O in class.

Simplistically, making Jell-O uses the same process as making steel. You mix ingredients, heat them up, and pour the resulting liquid into different shapes of molds, depending on what you want to use the finished product for. The children had read about the process in a few books, and we had role-played it. In both processes you go from solid to liquid, then back to solid. There's lots of science in the lesson.

In the Family Homework of December 7, I put out a call to the families to send in Jell-O molds. We received a nice variety.

The whole class participated in the process during Research Workshop—we just couldn't leave them out. What fun! Research Workshop was delicious that day.

Research Workshop: Looking at Coal and Steel Production Through Photographs (Days 32–36, with Irena and Paula)

During Research Workshop and often spilling over into Writing Workshop or Center Time, we studied the work of two social documentary photographers, Earl Dotter and my father, Milton Rogovin. We looked at copies of Dotter's photos of coal miners and my father's photos of steelworkers, then wrote about the photos on index cards that we displayed in the classroom.

Many of the steel mills in the United States have been closed for years, and many were moved to non-union areas or abroad. This issue is important to me, but I didn't think it should be a major focus for first graders. My father has documented the lives of steelworkers before and after Bethlehem Steel closed. We showed the children photos of the steelworkers, both women and men, and briefly discussed mill closings. I hope that the children will follow this particular issue in the future.

Share Time

After each of our workshops, the children shared their findings. Their research was now the domain of the whole class.

Extending the Research into Meeting

Finding Connections in Literature. Over the months of this research study, I read a number of stories about mining to the class at Meeting. One day, I read *In Coal*

Country, by Judith Hendershot. The story takes place in Diamond Grove, a coal town in Ohio. I let Jordan Nassau borrow the book. The next day, he hurried into class to tell me that his grandfather, a coal miner, had lived in Diamond Grove. Amazing!

Extending the Research Outside of the Classroom: Jordan Nassau's Trip

Some of Jordan Nassau's relatives are coal miners in the Pittsburgh area. Jordan did research about their work when he visited Pittsburgh for the holidays, then made a book that he shared with the whole class.

Figure 7–5. A page from Jordan Nassau's book about his trip to the coal mine in Pennsylvania.

Interviews

Just by asking families from our school, we found plenty of people to interview and lots of resources. The whole class conducted the interviews, with the children asking lots of questions and taking notes. It interested me that the children bought up the issue of unions and workers struggling to improve their working conditions again and again during the interviews.

It was important to me that the children learn about steelworkers of different nationalities and from different racial or ethnic groups.

After each interview, the children made pages for a homemade book, which we then used for guided reading lessons. These are the people we interviewed:

Barbara Abrash—November 30. Barbara is a professor of film at a nearby college and is Phoebe's aunt. We interviewed her briefly on Grandpeople's day. When our research about steel making began, Barbara sent in a movie she produced about coal mining in the former Soviet Union. She said it was for adults, but might have something in it for our class. When I previewed the film at home, I realized that it was way too complex for first graders. Since Barbara had gone out of her way to get the film to us, I wanted to find some way to use it. I showed the children two short segments about workers in the coal mines. We didn't use the audio because it was adult talk.

Raymond Oberdecker—December 15. Raymond, whose grandchildren Jessica and Andrew had been in my classes in the past, was the son of a coal miner in Pennsylvania. Raymond told us about life in a coal mining family. His father, Rudy, got up at 4:00 A.M. and went to work at 5:00. He was involved with worker safety, so he checked the timber that held the coal up and made sure no one took cigarettes or matches into the mine. And he checked the canaries to see if they were still alive. If all was well, the other workers could come into the mine.

The children asked Raymond if it was a difficult life. He responded, "We were kids. It was just life. That's the way it was." He brought photographs and books for us to look at, and also told us that his grandfather had been a coal miner in Austria.

Phil Batton—January 4. Phil's grandson, Nicholas, was a fifth grader at MNS. Nicholas hadn't been in my class, but I was a friend of his grandmother, Barbara. Because I had been talking about our vehicle research, Barbara told me about Phil, and arranged the interview. Phil is a retired teacher from an entire family of steelworkers in the Pittsburgh area. Phil told us that his grandfather and other family members were active in the union's efforts to win better health and safety conditions and better pay. We made a mural about the steel mill. (See Figure 7–6.)

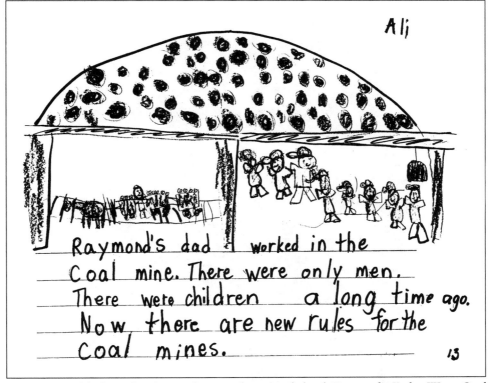

Figure 7–6. Ali Greenberg's page from our homemade book *Raymond's Father Was a Coal Miner, A Book About Jessica and Andrew Cannizzaro's Grandfather*. December.

Tom Fox—January 13. Christopher's father, Tom, who renovates apartments, wanted us to interview him at his work. I wanted to find a way to integrate his work into our study of vehicles, so I asked Tom to wait until we found the right time in our inquiry. We interviewed Tom at school, then he took us another day to see an apartment he was renovating. (See Figure 7–8.) We saw that each of the jobs of renovation is done by a different subcontractor. Jodi had said the same at her interview about building houses. The children could easily see that the concept of division of labor is similar in the production of steel for use in vehicles.

Monique Berkowitz—January 27. Ben's great-grandfather, Frans van Dorp, had been a coal miner in the Netherlands, where Ben's mother, Monique, was raised. She brought a photograph of her grandfather and a miner's lantern headlamp to show us. When the mines were closed in the Netherlands, the government worked with the union to train the miners for other jobs.

Figure 7–7. Phil Batton and Paula at the interview.

Extending the Research into Meeting

I had read *Night Comes to Steel Town*, by Anna Egan Smucker, earlier in the year and I read it again at Meeting after we interviewed Phil. The class was fascinated by the similarities between this story and Phil's. The book affirmed what Phil had told us and even provided additional information.

Extending the Research into Writing Workshop

Coal mining and steelworking poems and stories became a regular feature of Writing Workshop for all the children, not just those in the vehicle research group. All it took was for one child to write about a steel mill and then share the story with the class. After classmates' comments and questions, I complimented the author and suggested that others could write about the topic. I was thrilled to see such young children writing about such an important topic and looking at their writing gave me

Figure 7–8. Christopher Fox's quilt patch about his father, Tom. This patch is part of the People at Work quilt.

another way to assess their understanding of the topic and their developing writing skills.

Family Involvement

The excerpts from the Family Homework from December and January give a good idea of the other delightful experiences we had. I kept the families informed about our activities, telling them the names of the books we read, videos we saw, and photographers and other artists whose pictures we used for our research. Family members have often told me that they have gone out of their way to borrow or buy the same resources we use in the classroom. You can see from the Family Homework of December 7 that I share my strategies for finding new resources with families.

Figure 7–9. Ben Berkowitz's mother, Monique, at the interview. You can see the miner's lantern from the Netherlands.

Research Workshop: Production of Glass (Days 37–38, with Irena and Paula)

Our group chose to research how glass is made for use in vehicles. The level of interest in our research was still very high. A few new children had joined our group, and a few children had moved to other groups. But I wanted the formal study to end soon, so I decided to make our research about glass very brief, unless there was overwhelming interest from the children or we found possibilities for interviews or trips.

We talked about prior knowledge, our questions, and how we might find information. We looked in books I had found at the public library. We role-played the process of making glass for car windows. Right away the children observed that the process is similar to the one that's used to make steel, cake, and Jell-O: Ingredients are mixed, heated, and put into a mold. Although we had talked about solids, liquids, and gases in science, I chose not to make a big deal about glass being a liquid.

Share Time

The class was fascinated by the glassmaking process, and children added their prior information to the discussion.

Family Involvement

Families responded to my call for resources with books, samples, and interview contacts for us. The Family Homework of January 11 shows how I extended our classroom research into the homes by having the children search for ways glass is used at home.

Interview

George Greenberg—January 29. At times during the school year I take out the class survey I did at the beginning of the year. I had recorded information about jobs and hobbies to help me with planning. Sometimes the jobs listed at the beginning of the year don't seem relevant to us then, but become relevant later in the year. That's what happened with Ali's father, George.

How valuable that information proved to be when I thought about people to interview about glass production. I also remembered, from when Ali's brother Nicholas was in my class two years before, that George traveled around the world searching for companies that make products that are used for making lights or lamps. George would be perfect for our research. You can read the details of the interview in the Family Homework of February 1.

Reflecting on the Teaching

Finding People to Interview. Teachers may worry that they don't have the right people to interview. My approach is to take a closer look at my class families. Sometimes a survey doesn't give you enough information—for instance, a family member may just tell about a current job, not past jobs. They may not tell you about their talents or hobbies.

The more you communicate with the families, the more information you will uncover. You will find out about the parent or guardian and about their relatives, friends, coworkers, and other contacts. Family Homework and sending notes home can help you learn such information, but the best information usually comes through informal conversations in the classroom or schoolyard, or on the phone.

Research Workshop: A Culminating Project
(Day 39, with Irena and Paula)

As a culminating project to their research, the children made a car they could play in at Center Time, using a large cardboard box with plastic wrap for windows.

Share Time

Everyone wanted to see and play in the car—the class was delighted with it. Some children even helped the group paint the finishing touches at Center Time.

More Interviews

Robert Snyder—March 4. Months after our last formal workshop for research about People Who Make or Drive Vehicles, I met a father from my friend Isabel Beaton's kindergarten class. Isabel knew everything my class was doing, and knew I just had to meet Max's father, Robert Snyder. Robert had written a book, *Transit Talk,* that's filled with interviews of New York City bus and subway workers.

I was nervous before Robert visited our classroom because I thought what he talked about might be too far over the students' heads. I called Robert at home and asked him to be prepared to read the interviews in his book that would be most relevant to the children. That was a good idea—our interview with Robert turned out to be one of the best ever! Why? Because we learned that Robert and our class do exactly the same jobs:

- We both interview all sorts of people so we can get information.
- We both write about the interviews.
- We both share our information with others.
- We both work with museums to improve their exhibits (our art research group did that).
- We both learn about people who drive vehicles.

What a match. You could feel the children's excitement about the commonality as the interview moved along. Children kept saying, "Oh, we do that," "Oh, we know about that," and "We did research about that."

The children were practically rolling on the floor with enthusiasm when Robert read selected interviews from his book. We loved the story about the subway worker who helped a woman deliver a baby right there on the train.

The interview lasted over an hour and a half. You might think that's too long for first graders, but if you'd been there, you would have thought otherwise. The children and I were spellbound. It was one of those special moments in teaching that we always wish for.

Sometimes you can tell how good an interview was by the writing that is done afterwards for our homemade book. The children had so much to say after Robert's visit. They had seen themselves in his work. The homemade book was a way for me to assess the children's comprehension and writing skills.

Figure 7–10. Robert Snyder reading from his book, *Transit Talk*, at the interview.

Jimmy O'Sullivan—March 12. In January, when Ruth's mother, Carmel, heard that we would be studying about steelworkers, she rushed to tell me about her father. Jimmy had retired from his work at West Foundry in Ireland, where he lives. He would arrive in New York with his wife, Sheila, for St. Patrick's Day. This was long after our research group would have ceased meeting formally, but we were willing to wait. After all, we would be meeting, shaking hands with, and even hugging a *real* steelworker. We even learned a synonym for *steel mill—foundry*. When we did interview Jimmy, the children got to review the concepts we had learned earlier in the year.

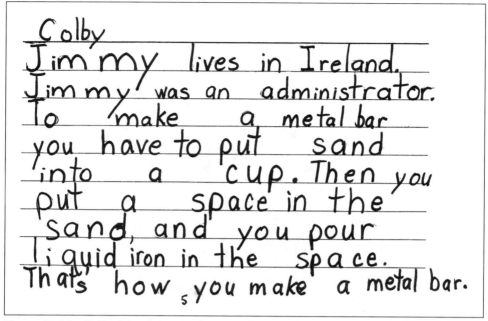

Colby

Jimmy lives in Ireland.
Jimmy was an administrator.
To make a metal bar
you have to put sand
into a cup. Then you
put a space in the
sand, and you pour
liquid iron in the space.
That's how you make a metal bar.

Figure 7–11. Colby Minifie's page from our homemade book *Sheila and Jimmy, An Interview of Ruth's Grandfather*. March.

Brenda Davis—May 3. Brenda's grandfather had been a coal miner in Nova Scotia, Canada. Her daughter, Isabelle, was a second grader at MNS. Isabelle hadn't been in my first grade, but parents talk—in the schoolyard and in a group that goes out to breakfast before work weekly. Word got out that my students were doing research about coal and steel, and that's how I came to meet Brenda.

This interview took place in May, long after our formal research group had ended because Brenda wanted to do more research before the interview. She brought photos, poems, and even a song about her grandfather. What a story Brenda told us! Her grandfather, William Davis, was in the famous miners' strike of 1920. The Canadian miner's holiday was named after him.

Reflecting on the Teaching

Did We Answer Our Original Questions? What did all of our activities have to do with vehicles? Were we straying too far from the topic? Let's go back to the original questions the children asked:

Who makes the vehicles?
What are they made from?
Where are they made?
Who drives them?

Yes, we did answer the questions. Our formal research study about People Who Make or Drive Vehicles lasted four and a half months, but informal study, including various interviews, continued until June. We could have finished more quickly if we had said that cars are made from steel, rubber, and glass and stopped there. But each of those materials is produced from other materials, and each material used in a vehicle is produced by many, many people. The starting point for many of the materials was far away from where we live.

Our research study started with *product* and had us first wonder about and then investigate the *process*. While looking at process, we wanted to know about the *people* who did each part of the process. Digging deep below the surface grabbed the children's attention. The detours and turns we made off the main road of our study is what made it so interesting to all of us.

You can see how far we strayed from a traditional textbook approach. To find out about the people who make or drive our vehicles, we really had to dig. As we dug, we found incredible resources. Just imagine meeting the son of a coal miner, a subway train operator, the granddaughter of a Canadian coal miner hero—all of whom were connected to our school! Our research study went from being a "nice" experience to being a profound one.

The children loved the role-plays and the stories we heard during interviews. They worked on a Lego assembly line, played in the coal mine, made Jell-O "steel," and painted murals. Children who might ordinarily be at the fringe of a class plunged right into the middle of the research. Research study is a very active way of learning, and an exciting way to learn and to teach. It gives us another way of looking at the world and making connections between what we see and learn . . . Wow, if you know that about cars and trucks and motorcycles, it's probably the same for everything we use.

Do the children really *know* about coal and steel production now? A little. You'd need to talk with them or read their poems and stories to find out. Would they pass a test about it? Perhaps. But will their fascination with the topic continue for years to come? For most of the children, yes. Our study was just the beginning. When they hear words like *rubber, latex, steel, steel mill, iron foundry,* and *steelworker* on the news, they will perk up and listen. That's what I want. And they have learned how to do research, a skill they'll be able to apply to anything they want to learn.

Summary of the Research Study About People Who Make or Drive Vehicles

Interdisciplinary Aspects

Writing

- developing note-taking skills at the interviews and at Research Workshop
- writing pages for our homemade books about the interviews
- writing related fiction and nonfiction during Writing Workshop and Center Time, and at home
- writing poetry about the topic
- writing about photographs
- writing labels and signs for murals and dioramas
- writing letters of inquiry and letters of thanks
- writing for related Family Homework assignments
- writing and producing a skit about the production of rubber
- editing and revising our writing

Reading

- doing word study and reading our homemade books in school and at home
- creating, reading, and using word webs about words in our homemade books
- reading books—fiction and nonfiction
- reading newspaper and magazine articles
- reading the labels and signs on our murals and using them to assist with reading and writing
- reading information on the Internet
- reading words from songs
- reading captions under photographs and pictures in books
- reading fact sheets, and brochures
- reading instructions for making a model car
- reading about the ingredients of steel and glass
- reading the recipe for making Jell-O
- learning to use our Word Wall
- adding key words from our research study to the Word Wall
- reading and reciting related poetry

Using Literature

- reading aloud related literature, both fiction and nonfiction
- discussing read-alouds
- reciting poetry

- looking for connections between literature and poetry and the research study

Art
- illustrating pages for our homemade books
- making sketches
- looking at photographs and pictures
- painting murals and posters
- creating a "coal mine"
- making a diorama
- making patches about the research study for the People at Work quilt
- creating a car from Legos
- making a model car
- creating hanging mobiles about cars
- creating a "video on paper" about rubber production
- building a cardboard car

Music and Dance
- singing and dancing to "Sixteen Tons" and other related songs

Science and Health Science
- learning about the production of rubber, steel, and glass
- learning about the formation of coal and minerals that are used to make steel and glass
- learning about solids, liquids, and gases
- learning about the effects of heating and cooling
- learning about environmental issues
- learning about health and safety issues
- learning about work-induced diseases such as black lung disease
- learning about rocks, fossils, and minerals
- learning about problems in the rain forests while learning how rubber is produced

Math
- using the topic of our research in story problems
- measuring ingredients for Jell-O
- counting, adding, and subtracting
- learning about different sizes and shapes of coal
- observing patterns in the subway stations and making our own patterns

Drama

- role-playing the production of rubber, steel, and glass during Research Workshop, at interviews, and at Center Time
- role-playing the work of coal miners in our block area at Center Time
- role-playing the assembly line using Legos
- role-playing workers' efforts to get better working conditions and job benefits
- writing and producing a skit about rubber production

Social Studies

- reading maps and atlases
- developing skills to conduct informal interviews
- developing skills to conduct formal interviews
- learning about the people who produce or drive vehicles—the people behind the product
- learning about people working cooperatively to produce a product
- learning about the role of unions in creating better working conditions and job benefits
- looking at issues that workers have in common
- looking at certain jobs as they were a long time ago and as they are today
- looking at people's efforts to save the rain forests
- creating bulletin boards of photographs, drawings, and collages to document the research
- checking sources of information

Multicultural Aspects

- interviewing people of different races and nationalities
- writing and reading homemade books about our interviews
- using books (fiction and nonfiction), magazines, and other resources with information about or pictures of people of different races and nationalities
- posting photographs of people of different races and nationalities who are involved in making and driving vehicles

Gender Issues

- interviewing both women and men
- writing homemade books about both women and men
- discussing the exclusion of women in the coal and steel industries, and how that changed
- discussing how women were excluded from driving public transportation and how that changed

- learning how language changes to reflect changes in thinking about gender issues; for example, how the job title for the driver of a subway train was changed from *motorman* to *train operator*
- using books (fiction and nonfiction), videos, magazines, and other resources that show both women and men producing vehicles and the materials used to make vehicles
- posting photographs of women and men in this field of work

Family Involvement

- family members arranging and participating in related interviews
- family members arranging and participating in trips
- families sending in resources such as books, videos, CDs, tapes, pictures, news articles, and coal and minerals from home and from public libraries.
- family members helping with Family Homework by doing observations, having discussions, doing the assignments, and doing projects
- family members participating in planning and assessment with the teacher and student teachers
- family members helping create patches for the People at Work quilt
- family members helping during Research Workshop and at other times during the day
- family members talking informally with the class about the research
- families and extended families helping with and attending the Family Celebration

Resources Used

- prior knowledge
- formal and informal interviews
- age-appropriate fiction and nonfiction books
- books for older children and adults, adapted for use with younger children
- newspaper and magazine articles
- songs
- brochures
- advertisements
- trips
- objects (rubber, steel, glass)
- raw materials (iron ore, coal, etc.)
- mining equipment (hard hats, lanterns, steel-toed shoes, train whistles)
- cooking
- the Internet

- videos
- photographs
- real vehicles
- unions
- artwork in the subway

8

Research Study: Woody Guthrie

Getting Started

In late September, Ben's mother, Monique Berkowitz, asked me what I thought about researching the folksinger Woody Guthrie as part of our research study of People at Work. She knew from the Family Homework of September 15 that some of the children wanted to do research about singers. Her husband, Steve, had met Woody's daughter Nora Guthrie at a music conference through his work. Monique suggested that Steve could help us make contact with Nora.

My heart jumped. Just the thought of a Woody Guthrie research study made me excited—and if teachers are excited about our work, the children will be, too, if we can find ways to pass on our enthusiasm.

We would start with what the children knew. They knew the song "THIS LAND IS YOUR LAND" and my adaptation of "SO LONG, It's Been Good To Know Yuh," which we sang every day at dismissal time. I knew lots more Woody songs from my childhood. I could certainly draw on my own life experiences.

Where else could I turn for help? Once my class decides on a research topic, I use the world as a resource. I told my parents, my brother and sister, my colleagues, friends, and families from former classes. I was sure they would have suggestions. Most importantly, I told the families in my class through the October 5 Family Homework.

Family Involvement

Why did I tell all of the families about our Woody Guthrie research study when the research group would be no more than ten children?

- The research of each group is the domain of the entire class.
- At the end of each Research Workshop, each research group shares what they have learned or done that day, so every child in the class would learn about Woody Guthrie.
- I wanted every child to learn as much as possible about Woody Guthrie at home. You want the parents, grandparents, and other relatives to tell their stories.

> Perhaps they know Woody Guthrie songs and will sing them with their children.
>
> Perhaps they have heard Woody Guthrie and will tell the family about that.
>
> Perhaps they have never heard of Woody and the child will teach them. There will be discussions at home.
>
> Perhaps they are from another country and heard "THIS LAND IS YOUR LAND" in their native language or in English. Some of Woody's songs are sung around the world. (A visiting principal from Canada joined us in singing this song, then, to our surprise, added a special verse they sing in Canada.)

- I wanted as many resources as possible for the research, both people and materials. If you tell all of the class families about a topic, you are sure to get a variety of resources.

Shortly after I sent home that Family Homework, the resources started pouring in. We received three books:

- *This Land Is Your Land*, by Woody Guthrie, illustrated by Kathy Jakobsen
- *Mail Myself to You*, by Woody Guthrie, illustrated by Vera Rosenberry
- *Grow Big Songs*, by Woody Guthrie and Marjorie Mazia Guthrie (a book and tape)

I begged my father to send me books about the Great Depression and the Dust Bowl, which Woody wrote many songs about.

I shared information from our Research Workshops, trips, and other activities with the families in the Family Homework from October 5, 19, and November 2. Each week, I tried to find ways to extend our research into the homes.

Reflecting on the Teaching

A Request from a Family Member Turns into a Major Research Study. Imagine that! Yes, the children wanted to learn about a singer. A parent had a suggestion that was relevant to our theme, People at Work, and that suggestion became our curriculum. What an empowering process this was for both the children and their families.

Who Was in the Research Group?

Most of the children in the group had chosen to join, plus there were two who I felt needed to be in my group because I knew they could get deeply involved with my help. Some of the children in the group had learned Woody's songs at home; some knew only the few songs they had learned in school. The children ranged from emergent readers to fluent readers.

Research Workshop: The Three Steps for Beginning the Research (Day 1)

The children and I gathered around Table Five. We began by singing a Woody Guthrie song that was new to them, "Wake Up." It was the first thing in the morning, so the song was appropriate. We laughed as we stretched and sang, "Stretch arms, stretch arms, stretch arms," and so on.

Tapping into Prior Knowledge

Then we talked about what the children already knew about Woody Guthrie. Most of them knew two of Woody's songs, but didn't know that he had written them. Ben knew Woody had a daughter named Nora, because his parents spoke about that at home. This information helped me know where to begin.

Asking Questions

I told the children a little bit about Woody Guthrie, then we made a list of their questions about him, which I wrote on a chart. I had some questions, but decided to save them for a later date.

> **Our Questions About Woody Guthrie**
> What songs did Woody Guthrie write?
> Why did Woody Guthrie write songs?
> Where did Woody live?
> Did Woody have children?

Thinking of Ways to Find Answers

We made a list of ways we could find answers. After being in the class only a few weeks, the children had already been in one research group and participated in several class interviews, so they had some good suggestions for resources:

Ask our families.
Ask Ben's father.
Ask Woody's children and grandchildren.
Read the newspaper.
Read books.
Watch a video.
Watch TV.
Look on the Internet.
Listen to Woody's music.
Think in our minds.

Probably the most important point on that list is "think in our minds." Using prior knowledge is the starting point for any research. To enhance our list of resources, I showed the children a brief biography about Woody at the end of the book *This Land Is Your Land*. I read a few paragraphs to give them a taste of Woody's life, and we talked about what we read. We read that Woody (Woodrow Wilson Guthrie) was born in Oklahoma in 1912, so we turned to the large map on the wall and found Oklahoma, then added the word *map* to our list of resources. Throughout Research Workshop we stopped so the children could take notes. Since it was so early in the year, we talked about what they could say in their journals and different ways they could record the information using pictures, words, or both.

Share Time

Near the end of Research Workshop, all the research groups stopped working and put away pencils and markers. The children moved so they would be able to see and hear each other. The children in the Woody Guthrie research group shared a few of their questions with the rest of the class and talked about some of the ways we would try to find information.

Making Plans

I wasn't sure how to begin answering the children's questions. I needed a hook, a way to begin the research study. I found no published or online study guides to refer to. Would we search through biographical information? Would we do a time line of Woody's life? I thought that might not work with my first graders.

Because Woody expressed his thoughts and feelings so brilliantly through music, maybe we should just turn to his music. Some of Woody's songs were lots of fun and some were very serious. Perhaps some of the songs were too complex for first graders. Which of the more serious songs could I bring into the classroom? This was an ongoing question for me.

The children's questions, family members' questions, my student teachers' questions, and my questions would become the basis for planning our research study. My thoughts turned to making the study interdisciplinary—the music part was easy, but what could we do in writing, reading, literature, math, science, art, and drama? This question would stayed on my mind as I listened, observed, and planned.

Research Workshop: Role-playing "SO LONG, It's Been Good To Know Yuh" (Day 2)

I decided that we would start with the songs we knew, breaking them down stanza by stanza so we would understand their meaning. As we went along, I would introduce new songs, the fun ones just for fun; the serious ones for their content.

Our first serious song would be "SO LONG, It's Been Good To Know Yuh," which is about farmers in the Great Plains region of the United States during the Dust Bowl of the 1930s, a period of a serious drought and economic depression.

We returned to the biography of Woody Guthrie in the back of the book *This Land Is Your Land*. We read that farmers in Oklahoma lost their crops because of the drought and the way the soil had been cultivated. Many people moved west to Texas and California to search for jobs. I knew that drought and crop loss were concepts my first graders didn't really understand because they weren't part of their life experience, so we did a role-play about a family losing their crops. As I narrated the story, I assigned children to different roles. They pretended they were farmers in Oklahoma more than sixty years ago. There was no rain for weeks and weeks and the land got so dry and the dust blew all over. The children role-played the wind.

I introduced a new stanza about the dust storm, talking it rather than singing it. We continued our role-play. The crops and farm animals died, and there was no work for the farmers. We talked about how they would feed their families and we discussed our feelings. Then we pretended we were the family, loading our belongings onto a car, saying good-bye to our friends and our land, and traveling west to look for new jobs. As we left, we sang the song we already knew, "SO LONG, It's Been Good To Know Yuh."

Over the years I had adapted this song for dismissal time. Instead of singing "This dusty old dust is a gettin' my home, and I've got to be drifting along," I had changed it to "See you tomorrow, it's time to go, we've got to be gettin' along." Now that we had learned and understood the real words, the children insisted that we use the real verse, which we did until the very last day of school.

This brief role-play let the children see that the biographical information in *This Land Is Your Land* would be useful in learning about Woody's life and his songs. We were learning how to use resources.

During the role-play, we stopped for discussions and for the children to take notes in their research journals. Taking notes at this early point in first grade meant drawing pictures, sounding out words, and copying certain key words I had written on the board, including *Woody Guthrie, drought, farm,* and *rain.*

Share Time

The children presented a few segments from their role-play to the rest of the class, which gave the entire class a chance to become acquainted with the issues in the song.

Reflecting on the Teaching

For Teachers of Older Children. Woody Guthrie's songs about the Dust Bowl open the door to many topics. Choosing the right topic to focus on depends on time factors and the age and interests of the children, families, and teacher. Science topics related to Woody's songs include

- the causes and effects of droughts
- how mishandling land leads to serious erosion
- irrigation and other solutions to droughts

Social studies topics include

- the economics of the Great Depression
- poverty and unemployment
- migration of people seeking employment

Extending the Research at Meeting

Every day at Meeting the whole class sang one or more Woody Guthrie songs, the fun ones and the serious ones. The children from the research group played a leadership role in explaining the meaning of the songs.

Research Workshop: Using Photographs to Deepen Understanding (Day 3)

We gathered again around Table Five to take another look at "SO LONG, It's Been Good To Know Yuh." I had found more verses in one of my favorite books of folksongs, *Rise Up Singing*, and had copied several onto a large piece of poster board. (I skipped verses that I thought weren't appropriate for first grade, the kind of choice you must make all the time when you use resources that weren't developed specifically for young children.) We sang the song.

My father, Milton Rogovin, is himself a social documentary photographer, and he has a great collection of the work of the social documentary photographers who worked for the Farm Security Administration during the Great Depression. I asked him to send me some of his books. I knew it would give him pleasure to know that young children were learning from the photographs.

I told the children that my father (then eighty-eight) had sent some books for our research. The children thought it was great that my father, who was *so old*, wanted to help us. They divided into groups to look at the photos in *An American Exodus: A Record of Human Erosion*, by Dorothea Lange and Paul Shuster Taylor and *Portrait of a Decade: Roy Stryker and the Development of Documentary Photography in the Thirties*, by Forrest Jack Hurley. The children sketched some of the photos in their research journals.

The photographs showed exactly what we had talked and sung about. There was such sadness in the people's faces. We talked about that sadness and about how it must have felt to have to leave your home and your friends. We paused for note taking. We thought about why Woody wrote "SO LONG." The children thought that he and the people who took the photographs had the same idea—to let the world know about a terrible problem. Perhaps people would do something about it if they knew.

Share Time

The children told the whole class about my father's books and showed them a few pictures of farm families during the time of the Dust Bowl.

Reflecting on the Teaching

Adapting Resources. How often do first graders look at books for high school or college students or for adults? Not often. The key to using such books is to adapt the material for younger children, to find what *is* useful to them in a particular book. In this case, the photographs and captions in the books were useful.

At home I had skimmed through the written material in the books to see what I could read directly or paraphrase for the children. It's essential that teachers be determined to find ways to make all sorts of resources accessible to children. If we aren't, the lack of age-appropriate resources will stop us from teaching about important topics.

Planning

I looked at home for Woody Guthrie sites on the Internet. Appropriate Internet sites for young children are ones that let them work independently or in small groups, ones with lots of illustrations and less-complex writing that's appropriate for newer readers. One of the most important sites I found for our research was the Woody Guthrie Foundation and Archives site. I was delighted, because I knew the site would help us get in touch with people who knew a lot about Woody, perhaps even his family members. Another important resource was the Library of Congress website. (See the bibliography for these and other resources for the study of Woody Guthrie.)

Research Workshop: Using the Internet to Find Information About the Dust Bowl (Day 4)

Our research group gathered around Table Five. I told the children that we would be looking again at "SO LONG, It's Been Good To Know Yuh." Perhaps we could learn even more about Woody through his song. Since someone had suggested a few days before that we could get information from the Internet, we would try that. I asked a child to type *dust bowl* into a search engine. Up came a listing of several sites. The children and I were so excited. We saw photos by the great social documentary photographers, and Farm Security Administration videos of the Dust Bowl. It was one of the first times I'd seen a video on the Internet, and the children could see that I was thrilled.

The children observed that this was the same information we had learned from the biography in *This Land Is Your Land*, from my father's books, and from the stanzas of the song itself. They were excited about making these connections and said things like

"Wow, a video!"
"That's what we saw in that book!" (by Dorothea Lange)
"I saw that picture before!"
"Oh, that's the Dust Bowl, like in our song!"
"That's what happened to Woody's family, we know that already."

Share Time

At the end of Research Workshop, our group was still sitting at the computer, bubbling with excitement and anxious to share our experience. During Share Time we showed the class a one-minute video of the Dust Bowl we had found.

Reflecting on the Teaching

Finding Connections. When children are able to make connections, to link things together, a teacher says to herself, "Ah, this is what it's all about." In this case, the children connected prior knowledge, music, our role-plays, a biography from a book, social documentary photography from a book, and video and social documentary photography from the Internet. Each source provided a piece of the information that, together, formed a new body of knowledge.

That's what Loris Malaguzzi and his colleagues at Reggio Emilia refer to as the "co-construction of knowledge" (Edwards, Gandini & Forman 1998). Malaguzzi says that the main role of adults is to "activate, especially indirectly, the meaning-making competencies of children."

Extending the Research into Meeting

That afternoon at Meeting we sang "THIS LAND IS YOUR LAND," "Wake Up," and our verse about the dust storm in "SO LONG, It's Been Good To Know Yuh." For the remainder of the school year, Woody Guthrie songs were an important part of Meeting.

Extending the Research Outside Our School: A Trip

Ben's mother, Monique, heard about an exhibit of the oil paintings from the book *This Land Is Your Land.* The show would be closing in a few days, and the illustrator, Kathy Jakobsen, would be at the show on October 6 and would be available to speak with our class. I would have preferred going later, after we had spent more time doing research about the song and Kathy's book. But what an opportunity—we couldn't pass it up.

So with very little notice, we planned a trip to the Miele Contemporary Folkart Museum, a small gallery in walking distance of our school. I asked if any family members would like to join us, and several parents did. We ate lunch in Central Park, then went to the gallery, where we squished inside for an interview. Most of the pictures from the book were on display. The children's exclamations when they recognized the pictures were a great thrill to Kathy. Then Kathy answered our questions:

- How did you get the idea for the book?
- Did you know Woody Guthrie?

- How did you get the information?
- How long did it take to do the paintings?

and more. . . .

Kathy told us about some of the details in the paintings, many of which were way over the children's heads. I stopped to interpret Kathy's statements for the children only when I thought it was important for them to know something particular.

Many people aren't used to talking with groups of young children. As when we use an adult book with young students, we must select the most important points and paraphrase or interpret for the children at an appropriate level.

The children thought it was interesting that Kathy had put her own children in the paintings. We talked about how you can do what you want when you are the painter or author.

I thought the interview would take too long if we stopped to take notes after each question, so when the interview was over and we had thanked Kathy, we gave the children about ten minutes to draw or write in their journals about what they had seen and heard. Then we headed back to school.

After the trip, we wrote formal thank-you notes to Kathy and to the owner of the gallery, giving the children two opportunities to see and use the letter-writing format.

Research Workshop: Painting a Mural About the Dust Bowl (Day 5)

Our research group looked at pictures in the books *The Bitter Years* and *This Land Is Your Land* to give us a better idea of the Dust Bowl and how families loaded up cars and headed west. Children sketched some of the photos in their research journals. Then we put a large sheet of butcher paper on an area of floor we had cleared and began to work on a mural about the song "SO LONG, It's Been Good To Know Yuh."

We talked about what would be in the mural, deciding to paint a farmyard with sand piled up against the house and a bike and other equipment sticking up out of the sand, much like the photos from the books we had seen. The children began by drawing with crayons.

Share Time

The children shared their sketches and the drawing for the mural with the class and explained what the picture showed.

Reflecting on the Teaching

Isn't This Too Political for Young Children? All teaching is political because all teaching involves choosing topics: Teachers must decide what to include and what to exclude. Teaching about Christopher Columbus involves making political choices. Which perspectives do we include? Did Columbus "discover" the New World, as most curriculum guides say, or did he steal the land from the Native peoples, as some alternative curriculum guides say? Will we look at different perspectives? Such are our political choices.

Research studies by their very nature require teachers and children to make many such decisions. In a Woody Guthrie study, do we limit the information to Woody's birth, his family, and where he lived? Do we select the fun songs, serious songs, or some of each? Do we talk about what influenced his songwriting? These are big decisions.

Research Workshop: Chit-Chat as We Paint (Day 6)

When our research group gathered again, we reviewed some of the photographs and completed our crayon drawing of the farmyard, then moved the mural to the painting area and stapled it to the wallboard. The children put on smocks and we talked about which colors we wanted to use and who would paint which section. It was crowded, but I was there painting along with the children and keeping things peaceful. We talked and sang quietly as we painted. This informal talk, which my colleague, Isabel Beaton, calls "chit-chat," is at the heart of making meaning and constructing knowledge.

Share Time

The children enjoyed sharing the mural and having the others guess what was sticking up in the sand.

Research Workshop: Making Meaning Through Mural Painting (Day 7)

We began work on a new mural of Woody's family loading up the car with mattresses, pots and pans, and a few toys. First we planned, and then we did the drawing. When you draw with crayon first, you can do lots of editing together.

As the children painted pots and pans and a few toys on the mural, we thought about how we might feel if this were happening to us. Some children had moved within the city, between cities, or from one country to another. They already knew about moving, but while there were similarities, this experience seemed very different. We wondered how it must have felt to leave home, the farm, and friends when you weren't sure of where you were going.

Share Time

We reviewed the issues we were talking about to give the whole class a deeper understanding. We showed the class our partially painted mural and invited other children to work on it at Center Time.

Extending the Research into Center Time

Letting the children work on the mural during Center Time the rest of the week meant that students who weren't in our research group could get involved. The children from the group explained things to the others. We sang and talked our way through the work. When the two murals were finished, the children wrote labels on paper that we then glued to the murals. I hung the murals along the windows, right near story circle. I often saw children looking up at the murals as we sang Woody's songs at Meeting.

Extending the Research into Writing Workshop

Our research topic had begun to find its way into Writing Workshop. Both Ben and Ashley wrote pieces about Woody Guthrie, Ben a book called *Wake Up*, a retelling of Woody's song, and Ashley a piece about the Dust Bowl. We shared their work with the whole class. I wanted to make a big deal about it because that would encourage other children to select topics from their research to write about.

Research Workshop: Making a Video (Day 8)

Ivana Espinet, who worked for a program at Teachers College at Columbia University, came each Monday for about forty-five minutes to teach our class how to make videos. I had been trying to think of a way to give her efforts greater meaning for the children, and decided to ask her to help us make a video about our Woody Guthrie research. Perhaps we could even send the video to Nora Guthrie.

Ivana was pleased with the idea, which helped her feel connected to our research. She and our child videographers taped me interviewing the children in the research group, who stood in front of their murals holding some of the books we used as resources. I asked them to explain the murals, and to tell Nora Guthrie why we would like her to come for an interview. Annelise said, "Nora, you're your daddy's daughter, so you know so much about him. So we think you should come for an interview."

Reflecting on the Teaching

Let the Inquiry Take Over Your Life. Research studies need to take over teachers' lives if we want them to take over our students' lives. Here are a few examples of how my teaching extended into my personal life:

- When I had a conference with my son Eric's teacher at Teaneck High School, Rhetta Maide, she showed me some of the projects her students had done about *The Grapes of Wrath*. I realized that my first graders and her high school students were studying the same topic. Rhetta let me borrow a book written by a group of her students, retelling *The Grapes of Wrath* as a picture book for children.
- One day I spoke with my friend Lisa Seigman, the Manhattan New School science teacher, about our Woody Guthrie research. She said, "Oh, I studied dance with Woody Guthrie's wife, Marjorie." I asked Lisa to stop by our room to tell the children about her experience.
- I talked about our Woody Guthrie research with other moms at my son's soccer game. Garren Orner said, "Oh, I went to school with Nora Guthrie." I tried to learn as much as I could from Garren.

The point is that, once you and the children have determined your research topic, you must put the word out to gather resources. Ask anyone. Ask everyone. Make the research part of your life.

Extending the Research into Meeting

I read the picture book by Rhetta Maide's students. We had a great discussion about the Dust Bowl and the song "*SO LONG, It's Been Good To Know Yuh.*"

Research Group: Inviting Nora Guthrie to Our School (Day 9)

The children were going to write to Nora Guthrie to invite her for an interview, so we gathered around Table Five to review letter-writing format. We talked about what we might say in our letters, which we would send to Nora with our video. It would have been easy for Ben's father or I to just write a letter or call Nora, but the children needed to be part of the process of finding resources.

Reflecting on the Teaching

Touching History. The video must have won Nora over, because the day she received it at the Woody Guthrie Foundation and Archives, she watched it with her colleagues, then called me at school at 3:30 P.M. Someone came calling for me in

Isabel Beaton's room: "Nora Guthrie is on the phone. It's Nora Guthrie. Really!" I ran to the phone so fast. Talking with Nora was for me like connecting directly to her father and his whole period of history. It was also like talking with a friend or a sister, as Nora is very friendly. She loved the video and couldn't wait to meet the children.

At the Woody Guthrie Foundation and Archives, Nora and her coworkers gather resources about Woody's life and work, prepare exhibitions, and produce tapes and CDs. Adults are constantly at the archives doing research. It was thrilling to Nora that such young children had been doing real research about her father.

We arranged a date. By the time the conversation was over, my colleagues had gathered around me in the office to hear the news. For those of us who love Woody Guthrie's music, Nora was a celebrity.

Research Workshop: Learning a Fun Song (Day 10)

Our research group decided to make a mural about Woody's song "Mail Myself to You." Ashley was our model. We traced around her on a large sheet of butcher paper and painted the outline to create a girl. During the next RESEARCH WORKSHOP we took some recycled wrapping paper and ribbon and loosely wrapped the girl in it.

During the weekend I had found stamps in my childhood stamp collection from every country represented in our class. The whole class glued the stamps on top of the girl's head, just as in the song. The children decided to nickname the girl "Country Girl," since the stamps represented so many countries.

Share Time

We displayed the mural and the words to the song for all to see. All through the year, when we sang that song, a child would run over and stand by the mural to remind us of the words.

Research Workshop: Role-Playing "Hobo's Lullaby" (Day 11)

On days when a student teacher wasn't in class, her research group could join another group. On this day, the athletes research group joined the Woody Guthrie group to discuss a song I sang to my own sons when they were babies, "Hobo's Lullaby." The song was written by Goebel Reeves, but Woody Guthrie sang and recorded it so many times that it is associated with him.

The children were already familiar with the topic of people looking for work. I gave them some simplified background information about the Great Depression,

Figure 8–1. "Country Girl," a mural about Woody Guthrie's song "Mail Myself to You."

explaining that there was a time when many, many people had lost their jobs and didn't have money to pay the rent or buy food and clothing. I skipped discussing the stock market crash, and other reasons for the massive unemployment because it would have been way over their heads. Then we talked about hobos, who traveled all over the country searching for work. Woody had traveled with hobos.

As I told a story about hobos, the children acted out the parts. They pretended that they didn't have jobs, and that there were very few jobs available. We talked about what it would be like to have no money to feed your family. We looked at a picture book of trains to find out more about boxcars. Then the children pretended to leave their families, climb onto the tops of trains or into boxcars, and go from town to town. We ended each part of the role-play with a discussion. We thought about why Woody may have sung this song—probably to let the world know about the problem in hopes that people would try to do something about it.

Since we had made murals to show the content of a few songs, this time I let the children decide what project to do about "Hobo's Lullaby." They voted to write a book about the song. We jotted down what we needed to write about:

- the problem
- hobos looking for work
- Goebel Reeves' and Woody Guthrie's dream

Research Workshop: Creating a Book About a Song (Days 12–13)

The table was covered with books on trains. The children knew where to find the books, as each type of book had its own area in our classroom with a child-made label. Nearby was a chart tablet with the words to "Hobo's Lullaby." After we decided who would do each topic, the children took sketch paper and markers and began their work. They spread out, using two tables and the floor. When the drawings were finished, the children wrote using approximated spelling. If it had been later in the year, when their spelling was closer to standard English, they would have done all the writing, and I would have edited with them to put their words into standard English. But this was early in the year, and their spelling was generally far from standard English. After school, I translated their spelling into standard English so this could become a reading book.

Extending the Research into Reading Workshop

"Hobo's Lullaby" was our reading lesson. I placed the chart tablet on the easel so we could see how many different ways apostrophes were used in the song. The children came up and circled them. We found:

'bout
Hobo's Lullaby
don't
can't
that's
you're

Jordan Corbin said, "Woody was a letter skipper!" What a great observation.

We looked at the contractions and the abbreviations. We then practiced using the apostrophe to show ownership. I wrote on the board:

Hobo's Lullaby
Lilli's cat
Alex's dog

and more, using the children's names.

The children observed that the song sounded like a poem that rhymes. We also found a compound word in the song, *boxcar*. We added many of the words from this lesson to our Word Wall.

Extending the Research into Writing Workshop

To integrate our research studies into our Word Wall, we placed basic sight words such as *and*, *the*, *about*, and *because* on index cards as we found them in our reading, then placed the index cards under the appropriate letter of the alphabet on the Word Wall. We added key words that were related to interviews, trips, or other aspects of our research. Having key words on a Word Wall helps children write those words in standard English and edit their own writing.

So our Word Wall had a combination of high-frequency words and words key to our Woody Guthrie research, such as *friendship*, *drought*, *hobo*, *musician*, and *guitar*.

Research Workshop: Writing a Skit About a Song (Day 14)

Our Family Celebration would be upon us in a few weeks and each research group was preparing a presentation about its work. I thought that a short play would be more interesting than just telling what we had learned about Woody Guthrie, so we set out to write a skit about "SO LONG, It's Been Good To Know Yuh." We went through the song line by line, tossing around ideas for the play. I jotted the children's suggestions down in my journal.

Share Time

We let the rest of the class know that we were working on a skit about "SO LONG, It's Been Good to Know Yuh."

Research Workshop: Revising the Skit (Day 15)

It's tough to write a skit with a large group of children, so I brought my journal home at night and played around with the children's suggestions. I decided to make some of the lines rhyme, as so many of Woody's songs do. The next day, the children revised the lines. Then we made copies of the script for the children and we read them as a reading lesson. The children were thrilled to see their thoughts in script format. We had a great time practicing the skit in our Research Workshops until the day of the Family Celebration.

Share Time

We showed the class our script for the play. (You can see the script at the end of this chapter.)

Reflecting on the Teaching

Creating Resources About Topics That Are "Off the Beaten Path." Drama is a fantastic tool for making a topic part of children's hearts and souls and for teaching others. There are commercially available plays for almost every occasion, but there are few plays for children on topics that are "off the beaten path." There are no children's plays about Woody Guthrie, labor unions, and child labor. With this lack of resources, the only way we can present plays about some of our research topics is to write our own.

It is important that we share our homemade plays with other teachers and that we encourage them to write plays with their classes. I traded plays with teacher friends for years. One day, I typed up the plays and created a booklet that I had reproduced. It included plays my classes had written about Harriet Tubman, Paul Robeson, Martin Luther King, Jr., Nelson Mandela, and others. To this day, other teachers use or adapt those plays. Why not produce your own book of plays?

Interview: Nora Guthrie—November 10

The highlight of our research was interviewing Nora Guthrie, Woody's forty-eight-year-old daughter. Family members had purchased flowers and prepared snacks for the event. Seven mothers from our class and one from my former class came for the interview. The adults may have been even more excited than the children—some of us had sung Woody's songs when *we* were growing up. I hugged Nora as if she were my sister.

Nora had many stories to tell. The research group performed our play for her, and we sang together. There were some difficult moments, like when the children asked Nora how her father had died. She explained that he had been very ill with Huntington's disease, a degenerative illness, for many years. I translated that important information into first-grade terms so that we could discuss it. I don't like young children to be frightened, and perhaps the best way to keep them from being frightened is to provide hope, which Nora did by explaining that her family is working with other people in the Huntington Foundation to raise money for research to cure Huntington's disease.

We asked Nora to tell us about hobos. Nora told us that her dad said that although hobos had a difficult life, they had each other, they had friendship. She said that Woody had taught her that friendship is more important than *things*. Then she said that friendship is more important than Nintendo, and video games, and lots of other things. The children were stunned—many of them have Nintendo and many other games and toys. This was a moment to treasure. I stopped Nora so that we could discuss the significance of her statement for our lives. What she had said came up over and over until the end of the year.

Nora had great stories about Woody's kindness and generosity. She told us about the container of coins her family had on the table. Woody placed a sign on it that said something like "Dear Robber, if you need this money more than we do, please take it." Nora said that Woody would give his new warm winter coat to a stranger. Nora discussed the origin of some of his fun songs and the role her mother, Marjorie, played in his life.

Nora seemed pleased that the children knew so much about her father and about the issues in his songs. I was so proud of them. What a day!

Figure 8–2. Woody Guthrie's daughter Nora at the interview.

Reflecting on the Teaching

Touching History. How often do young schoolchildren have the opportunity to meet people right out of history books? Rarely. Over the last few years, my class has interviewed Nora Guthrie; Rachel Robinson, the wife of Jackie Robinson; Dr. Norman Latimer, the granddaughter of Lewis Latimer, who developed the filament for the light bulb; Carlton Green, former member of the Harlem Globetrotters; and others. These are real people who live amongst us.

You need not focus on celebrities for your interviews, but if famous people or their relatives are accessible, why not reach out to them? All you need is an address or name of the organization a person works with, which is often available on the Internet. Or maybe someone you know knows someone who knows someone. Ask the children's families and your colleagues to help. Be bold.

Extending the Research into Meeting

What Nora had said about friendship was fantastic. Meeting was a good time for children to share their work from Writing Workshop about friendship. We role-played several issues about friendship and keeping friends, a particularly difficult thing for some first graders. We acted out people doing negative things: not letting a friend answer a question, pushing, not giving a friend space. We laughed at our role-play and tried to figure out what was wrong. Then we did the role-play again, this time doing the right thing.

Social Action

The children internalized the concerns about social issues Nora Guthrie had raised. Soon after, when a hurricane devastated areas in South America, the children were quick to propose sending food and clothing. We joined other classes in taking up a collection.

Research Workshop: Turning a Special Moment into a Mural (Day 16)

Our Woody Guthrie research group gathered to write a formal thank-you letter to Nora. Lilli's mother, Tricia, had talked with Nora and found out that they both worked in the same building. What a coincidence. Tricia would deliver the letter for us. Then we made plans to create a mural about Woody giving his coat to a stranger. Other children from the class would help complete the mural at Center Time.

Share Time

We read our thank-you letter to the class. Later, everyone would get to sign it. We asked for help with the mural.

Figure 8–3. Our mural of Woody Guthrie giving his coat to a stranger.

Extending the Research into Meeting

To keep our discussion of friendship alive, we read and talked about the friendship poems we knew and learned some new ones, including "Poem," by Langston Hughes, "Two Friends," by Nikki Giovanni, and "Making Friends," by Eloise Greenfield.

Research Workshop: Writing a Homemade Book (Day 17)

The children usually write a page for our homemade books on the same day as an interview, but our interview with Nora was too late in the day. The next morning, the whole class gathered to review the interview and to think of topics for the pages in the book. They checked their interview journals for possibilities. I was happy to see that many children wrote about the concepts that were emphasized at the interview—sharing, helping, and friendship.

For the children who wrote most of their words in standard English, we edited together. I took their pages home and wrote over the children's words that weren't dark enough for the copier. For the children who used a lot of approximated spelling,

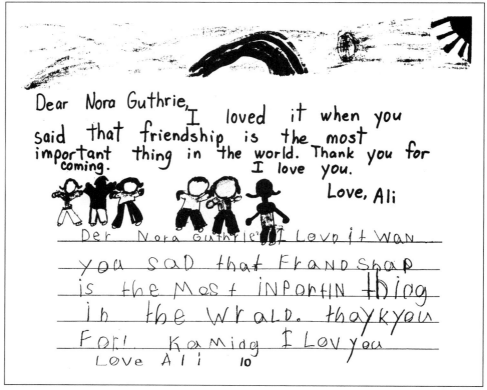

Figure 8–4. Alexandra Greenberg's page from our homemade book *Our Interview of Nora Guthrie*. November.

I copied their sentences into standard English on another part of the page. This way we could use the homemade book for reading lessons.

Extending the Research into Reading Workshop

The children made predictions about what words they would find in our homemade book about the Nora Guthrie interview. They predicted they would find *hobo, music, train, stranger, coat,* and several other words. Predicting what will be in a book or article makes reading much easier. Because I had spent so much time preparing the book, I was familiar with the content and had developed an informal plan for the reading lesson. I knew that some words would be sight words that the children copied into their reading journals. Others would be used to develop phonemic or language awareness. For example, the word *coat* had an *oa* spelling that we had seen in other books. We made a list of *oa* words, with the children suggesting words. As children made predictions, I quickly decided what to do with each word. For example, when a child predicted we would find the word *coat,* we no-

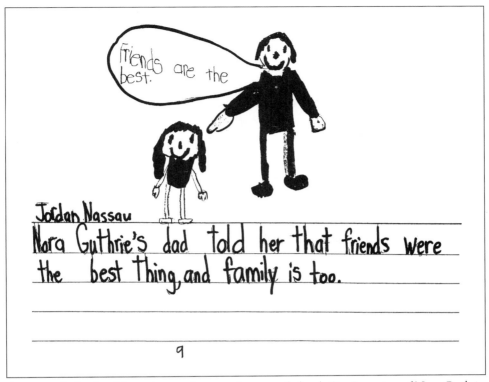

Figure 8–5. Jordan Nassau's page from our homemade book *Our Interview of Nora Guthrie*. November.

ticed that *coat* had an *oa* spellling. If the word they suggested didn't have the *oa* spelling, like *bone* or *bowl*, I wrote it on another part of the board anyway so they could see its spelling. We took the word *music* and looked at its other forms:

music
musician
musical
musically

We made a word web with the word *sing*:

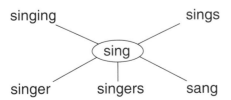

There were lots of surprises with our word webs, such as in this one, where *sing* changes to *sang*. I posted the word webs in the classroom so the children could refer to them during Writing Workshop. As a reminder to use word webs, I would ask the children where they could find a particular word in our room.

The children loved this word study. It was a fun and lively time, with very active participation. The first day, the children circled the words we had discussed in their copies of the homemade book. The second day, we made more predictions and did more word study. In preparation for reading the homemade book, we discussed strategies the children could use if they came to a difficult word. They reviewed a few strategies:

- Look at the pictures.
- Sound it out.
- Remember where they had seen it before.
- Skip the word, saying "mmmmmmmm" instead. Finish reading the sentence. Look back at the word to try to figure out what it might be. Check your guess. Does it have the right letters? Reread the sentence. Does it make sense?

The children read the book with a partner. After reading, they placed the books in their mailboxes so they could take them home and read them for Family Homework.

Family Involvement

By including the homemade book in the Family Homework for the week of December 7, the children had an opportunity to read out loud with a family member. They got to work on reading strategies. Just as important, the families became familiar with the content of the interview and could discuss the important issues.

Research Workshop: A Formal Rehearsal of the Skit (Day 18)

Our research group practiced the skit in the auditorium. We used the murals we had painted earlier for scenery.

Share Time

Each research group shared its presentation with the whole class.

Family Involvement

Our People at Work quilt was a class project. Several parents and I met before school in the classroom and talked on the phone to plan the quilt. On November 6, we had our first quilting bee. The children used fabric crayons to make quilt patches of the people we had interviewed and of research topics. The family members helped. Here are some of the patches they made about our Woody Guthrie research:

- Woody giving his coat to a stranger
- the interview of Nora Guthrie
- Kathy Jakobsen
- "Wake Up, Wake Up"
- "Hobo's Lullaby"
- "Mail Myself to You"

Figure 8–6. Elwin Walker's patch about the interview of Nora Guthrie. This patch is part of the People at Work quilt.

Research Workshop: Turning a Woody Guthrie Song into a Book (Day 19)

I typed up a few of Woody's fun songs at home, using a picture-book format. The children illustrated the song "Put Your Finger in the Air" while I helped a student teacher with her group's play. We would use the illustrations to make a new book for our library.

Share Time

The children shared their pages for the book *Put Your Finger in the Air*.

Research Workshop: Singing the Fun Songs (Days 20–24)

We practiced our play, then learned a fun song called "Howdi Do" from the *Grow Big Songs* tape that Ben's mother, Monique, had sent to school.

Share Time

We introduced "Howdi Do" to the whole class. We would sing it again later at Meeting.

Extending the Research into Writing Workshop

At Writing Workshop, Annelise started work on her new book, *SO LONG, It's Been Good To Know Yuh*, a retelling of our skit. Of course, she wrote "by Woody Guthrie, retold by Annelise. We celebrated her new writing. I have debated with myself and colleagues about whether it's appropriate for children to retell a play, skit, story, or song. I believe that it's a wonderful way for children to work on writing skills without having to make up a story, too. It can help children:

- remember things in sequence,
- learn how to retell and include the main events as well as details,
- work on using punctuation,
- work on special writing formats, such as the format for a play,
- review content,
- save the experience for the future, and
- learn to give credit to the original writer.

Family Involvement

It was November 24, the day of the Family Celebration. The children were so excited. We had a dress rehearsal and got set up for the evening celebration.

Before the children performed, I asked the audience who had done research when they were in first grade. The only people who raised their hands in this group of over 125 were children.

All the research groups presented something about their work. Our Woody Guthrie skit was well received. I played my guitar and led the audience in singing "SO LONG, It's Been Good To Know Yuh" and "Hobo's Lullaby." My oldest son, David, led everyone in singing "THIS LAND IS YOUR LAND." There were many tears. After the program we had a feast prepared by the families and me. It was a marvelous evening.

Social Action

On November 25, our research groups did a presentation for eight classes from our school. The children felt great about presenting their work to their peers and teaching them about a person as important as Woody Guthrie.

Reflecting on the Teaching

When the Children Glory in Their Learning. Our Woody Guthrie study took place early in the year. Near the end of June, Eliana and Chelsea picked up our book *This Land Is Your Land* to reread it. What they noticed during their rereading would make any teacher dance for joy. The girls came running over to where I was sitting. They were bursting.

"Paula, look what we found in this book. Look, here are people picking peaches like Alicia did." (Alicia Perez worked for the United Farm Workers. She told us about picking peaches in California when she was six years old.)

"Look, there are some people picking strawberries." (Alicia was organizing support for the strawberry workers at Driscoll Farms in California.)

"Look, there are some hobos on a train like in the song 'Hobo's Lullaby.'"

The two girls could hardly stand still. And there was more.

"Look, there are some homeless people, remember from "This Land Is Your Land." (There is a verse about people who go to the relief office, and we had read *Uncle Willie and the Soup Kitchen*, by Dyanne Disalva-Ryan and Mira Reisburg.)

"Look, there are some people doing child labor."

Eliana and Chelsea recognized so much that was related to our research. They knew I was delighted. I suggested they write a list of the topics they had recognized. The next day, during Writing Workshop, I suggested they turn their information into a book, and they did.

Why was this experience so special to the girls and me? We had learned such a wealth of information and thought about so many issues during the year in the process of answering our questions. It seemed as if Woody's concerns about humanity dovetailed with the other topics in our research studies. We seemed to have so much in common with him. I shared my thoughts with the two girls, who agreed.

At Meeting I reread *This Land Is Your Land* to the class. Chelsea, Eliana, and I pointed out the pictures that related to our research, and the whole class experienced a thrill of recognition and the pleasure of feeling that we had learned so much. The girls read their homemade book to the class. They felt great.

On the Friday before school ended in June, we sat in a circle and recounted memories of our year in first grade. Eliana said, "I remember the first day of school when we sang 'THIS LAND IS YOUR LAND' with the parents." Ben said, "I remember the first day of school when we thought about research topics and I said 'singers.'"

Summary of the Research Study About Woody Guthrie

Interdisciplinary Aspects

Writing
- developing note-taking skills at the interview and at Research Workshop
- writing a page for our homemade book about the interview
- writing books about Woody Guthrie at Writing Workshop and Center Time, and at home
- writing poetry about Woody Guthrie
- writing labels and signs for murals
- writing letters of invitation and letters of thanks
- retelling Woody Guthrie's songs in writing
- writing for related Family Homework assignments
- writing and producing a skit about one of Woody's songs
- editing and revising our writing

Reading
- doing word study and reading our homemade book in school and at home
- creating, reading, and using word webs about words in our homemade book
- reading the labels and signs on our murals and using them to assist with reading and writing
- reading information on the Internet
- reading words from songs
- reading captions under photographs and pictures in books
- reading newspaper articles about the Dust Bowl and Woody Guthrie
- reading books about Woody Guthrie, his songs, and the topics of his songs.

- learning to use our Word Wall
- adding key words from our research study to the Word Wall
- reading and reciting related poetry

Using Literature
- reading aloud related literature, both fiction and nonfiction
- discussing read-alouds
- reciting poetry
- looking for connections between literature and poetry and the research study

Art
- illustrating pages for our homemade books
- making sketches
- painting murals
- filming a real video
- looking at social documentary photography
- looking at paintings and drawings in books
- looking at paintings by Kathy Jakobsen in an art gallery
- making patches about the research study for the People at Work quilt

Music
- singing Woody Guthrie songs during Research Workshop, Meeting, dismissal, and the Family Celebration
- listening to tapes and records of Woody Guthrie's music, sung by him and by others
- doing research about the content of the songs
- singing along with Nora Guthrie

Science and Health Science
- discussing droughts
- reading about droughts in the newspaper
- learning about the Dust Bowl
- discussing the dust storm's impact on people's health

Math
- using the topic of our research in story problems
- looking at the dates when events occurred
- thinking about the past and the present

Drama
- doing role-plays during Research Workshop and our interview of Nora Guthrie

- writing and producing a skit about Woody Guthrie
- role-playing songs by Woody at dress-up during Center Time

Social Studies

- reading maps and atlases
- developing skills to conduct informal interviews
- developing skills to conduct formal interviews
- thinking critically about issues raised by Woody and Nora Guthrie, such as unemployment and homelessness
- developing concepts such as friendship, caring, and social action
- making connections
- checking sources of information
- creating a bulletin board of photographs, drawings, and writing to document the research
- collecting books for a local hospital
- collecting food and clothing for hurricane victims

Multicultural Aspects

- discussing Woody Guthrie's concern for people of all races and nationalities
- focusing on Woody's songs that are about people of all backgrounds
- asking people of all races and nationalities about Woody Guthrie
- using books with pictures and photographs of people of different races and nationalities
- singing songs about peace and friendship among all people
- combating misinformation, stereotyping, and prejudice

Gender Issues

- discussing Woody Guthrie's wife, Marjorie, with their daughter Nora
- using books and other resources with pictures and photographs of both women and men

Family Involvement

- family members helping to arrange and attending the interview of Nora Guthrie
- families sending in resources such as books, videos, CDs, tapes, pictures, and news articles from home and from public libraries
- family members helping with related Family Homework discussions and assignments
- family members participating in planning and assessment with the teacher and student teachers

- family members helping the children make patches about the Woody Guthrie research study for the People at Work quilt
- a parent delivering mail to Nora Guthrie
- family members helping during Research Workshop
- family members and friends talking informally with the class about Woody Guthrie
- families and extended families helping with and attending the Family Celebration

Resources Used

- prior knowledge
- a short biography of Woody from the back of the book *This Land Is Your Land*
- a formal interview with Nora Guthrie
- informal interviews with people who saw Woody Guthrie or knew Nora or her brother, Arlo Guthrie
- Woody's songs
- books made from Woody's songs
- biographical information about Woody from record, cassette, and CD covers
- videos
- the Woody Guthrie Archives in New York City
- the Internet
- books and newspaper and magazine articles meant for high school students and adults, adapted for use with younger children
- photographs and pictures
- the Woody Guthrie postage stamp
- records, tapes, CDs

Script from the Skit Written by the Research Group

SO LONG, *It's Been Good To Know Yuh*

A skit about Woody Guthrie's song "SO LONG, It's Been Good To Know Yuh," by Paula's research group: Ben Berkowitz, Simon Guzman, Annelise Stabenau, Ashley Beckford, Jordan Corbin, Paulina Koladzyn, and Paula Rogovin.

NARRATOR: Not a drop of rain.
Not one drop of rain
For months and months.

MA AND PA: This ground is so dry.
      If it doesn't rain soon
      All the corn and wheat will die.
CHILDREN: We're so hungry
      We want something to eat.
MA AND PA: There's no corn
      There's no wheat
      There's nothing to eat.
ALL: Nothing at all to eat.
(Make the sound of the wind.)
ALL: *(Sing Woody Guthrie's song)*

    A dust storm hit,
    And it hit like thunder.
    It dusted us over.
    Covered us under.
    Blocked out the traffic
    and blocked out the sun.
    Straight for home all the people did run.

ONE CHILD: Our cow is dead!
      She's there in the shed!
ALL: Now, there's no milk to drink
    No food to eat.
    This dusty old dust
    Blows from our heads to our feet.
MA AND PA: Let's take all our things
      And go out west.
CHILDREN: Maybe you'll find a job
      In California.
      That will be the best.
MA AND PA: So, let's load the truck. *(They pretend to load the truck that is in a mural in the background.)*
ALL: Hope we have better luck.
MA AND PA: Now, let's say good-bye.
ONE CHILD: I'm gonna cry.
ALL: Goody-bye, good-bye.
(Sing)
So long, it's been good to know yuh (3 times)
And I've got to be drifting along.

Appendix

Excerpts from Family Homework

Keeping in Touch with the Families

These are excerpts from the Family Homework bulletins I sent home in 1998–99. Each bulletin was four to five pages and included announcements, a review of the past week's work in all curricular areas, a projection of what would be happening the next week, and some homework assignments. Because of the length of these bulletins, I am including only excerpts here. Ellipsis points within square brackets [. . .] show where something has been left out.

Letter to Families—September 9, 1998

September 9, 1998

Dear Families of Class 1-407,

Welcome to our first-grade class. I'm looking forward to working with you because I consider YOU so important to your child's learning and development. You are my coworkers. Together, we have so much to offer the children.

I want to encourage your participation in our class activities. There are lots of ways for you to get involved with our class and in the school. I know that many of you are working full time or have younger children at home, so I will make every effort to find a variety of ways you can get involved. Here are a few ways you can get involved:

- Parents, grandparents, guardians, and other family members are welcome to work in our classroom. You may want to come to class daily, a few times a week, a half-hour before you rush off to work, on a day off, or whenever it is most convenient for you.

- You are welcome to help us arrange trips and to join us on trips.
- Your child will receive Family Homework every Monday in a blue folder. Please send the blue folder back to school every day. In the Family Homework you will find out what we have done in school the previous week, what topics and issues we have raised, whom we have interviewed, and so on. Then I will tell you what we will be doing in the coming week. I will ask you to discuss issues with your child. There will be two or three homework assignments that will be due on that Friday.
- This is homework for your family to do *with* your child. While I want you to help, the actual writing or drawings must be done by your child. I check the homework over the weekend and return it on Mondays.
- You are welcome and encouraged to help our class by sending in resources for our thematic study about People at Work. We will need books, magazine and newspaper articles, computer programs, music and art, videos, etc. Next week in the Family Homework I'll let you know more about our specific issues. If you want the materials to be returned, please put your name on them. Thanks.
- I want to encourage you to join the Parent-Teacher Association. There's lots of work to be done for book fairs and other schoolwide events. Also, the PTA conducts workshops about special issues. At the meetings, you can raise issues of concern to you.

For those of you who don't know me, this is my sixth year at Manhattan New School. I taught for twenty years in two schools in Washington Heights. My three sons are David (age twenty-three), Steven (age twenty-one), and Eric (age sixteen). So you can see, I've had lots of experience as a parent, too.

Over the years I have been active in the childcare and the antiapartheid movements and in efforts to make this a better world for all. In our class, we stress cooperation, people helping each other and being decent to each other. Fighting and meanness are unacceptable. If we want peace in the world, I believe we need to begin at home and in school.

I look forward to a wonderful year.

Sincerely,

Paula Rogovin

Family Homework—September 9–11, 1998

❖ *Social Studies*

Our theme this year will be People at Work. The children will do research about the many different jobs people do in this country and around the world. We will do research about barriers to work (jobs that were or are closed to people because of their race, gender, or disabilities). We will even examine the issue of child labor.

I want your children to feel free to ask questions. I want them to think of themselves as researchers. Also, we will search for ways to find answers to our questions. We will use books, computers, news articles, interviews, and so on to find answers. And we will go on many trips.

YOU, the families, will be one of our primary sources of information. I hope to schedule interviews with as many family members as possible during the year so that we can learn from you. If you have friends or acquaintances whose work would be interesting to the class, please let me know. If you have any resources for our thematic studies, please send them in. This might include pictures, books, uniforms, magazines, etc. [. . .]

Family Homework—Week of September 15, 1998

❖ *Social Studies—People at Work*

[. . .]

Last week when we discussed our theme of People at Work, the children expressed an interest in learning more about the work of *dancers, singers, athletes,* and *people who make or drive cars, trucks, trains, buses, airplanes, and other vehicles.* This week we will begin a few of the research groups.

Research Groups

Dance and Dancers. Our student teacher, Pam Wen, from Teachers College, will work with the dance research group.
[. . .]

People Who Make or Drive Vehicles. I will be working with this research group. If you have any resources or know anyone who is involved with making vehicles, please let me know. Chelsea's father, Stephan, is a train operator in the subway. We will interview him. You are welcome to join us for that interview. [. . .]

> √ *Your help is needed with this research.* We will need all kinds of resources, such as books, news clippings, pictures, work uniforms, videos, computer programs,

names of people we can interview about these topics, and places we can visit. If you want us to return any materials, please put your name on them. [. . .]

During Research Workshop children automatically get their research journals and bring them to their research group. During the workshop, I stop for children to take notes. In the beginning of the year, I may write something on the board or on a chart tablet, or the children will use approximated spelling. Later in the year when the children's writing is more fluent, children will take notes constantly without my having to stop for note taking. Note taking is an important skill. It serves several purposes:

- It helps children process the information.
- It supports children's effort to retain information.
- It helps improve writing.
- We can refer back to notes from a previous day. [. . .]

Family Homework—Week of October 5, 1998

❖ *Social Studies—People at Work*

Interviews

Last week we had two terrific interviews. On Monday we interviewed Chelsea's father, Stephan, who is a train operator. Stephan told us that people doing the job of driving the subway train used to be called *motormen*. Because many women drive subway trains now, the job is called *train operator*.

Can you help us think of other job titles that were changed, such as *mailman* to *letter carrier*, *policeman* to *police officer*? Please send us any you think of.

Stephan brought tools and equipment to the interview. He brought the vest that is used when a worker gets out of the train to look at the tracks.

We role-played what train operators do when there is a delay, such as when a drawbridge won't close or there is garbage on the tracks. This was very informative.

We saw Stephan's route on a subway map. The L line is gray on the map. Families, if you can get us copies of the subway map when you are on the subway next time, please send them in. Thanks. Stephan, thank you. [. . .]

√ Please discuss this interview with your child.
√ On October 28 we will meet Stephan at the L train at 8th Avenue and 14th Streets at 10:40 A.M. [. . .] Family members are welcome to join us for this adventure. We will have lots of adults with us to make sure that the children are safe. [. . .]

Last Tuesday we interviewed Jordan Nassau's family friend, Jennifer. Jennifer is a Rockette. It was so interesting to learn about how the Rockettes do everything in unison. Jennifer told us that the most important things for doing everything exactly the same are *to focus or concentrate, to work together* (not just do your own thing), and *to practice*. We role-played an audition and realized that it was very similar to the tryout Julie's father went to when he wanted to join the United States Select Soccer Team. Jennifer taught us some dance steps.

After the interview we went into the auditorium, where Jennifer showed us how to do the shim-sham. [. . .] Thank you, Donna, for arranging this interview.

√   Please discuss this interview with your child.

Research Groups

Dance and Dancers. Last week this group did research about dance shoes. If you have any old dance shoes or slippers you would like to lend us, please send them to class. This week Pam will be putting a Chinese folktale to dance. [. . .]

People Who Make or Drive Vehicles. Our new student teacher, Karen, is working with this group. They were discussing and role-playing the concept of a production line or assembly line. [. . .]

Annelise's mother, Denise, helped some children make a model car. Thanks, Denise.

Woody Guthrie. When we needed to form a new research group, Ben's parents, Monique and Steve, suggested that we do a study of the folksinger Woody Guthrie. I know that some of the families in our class grew up on Woody's music (as I did), and other families are not familiar with Woody's music. Perhaps some people know Woody's songs but didn't realize that he wrote them. For example, Woody wrote "THIS LAND IS YOUR LAND," "SO LONG, It's Been Good To Know Yuh," "Clean-O," "Put Your Finger in the Air," and more.

This research group started by making a list of ways we can learn about Woody. Perhaps more important than learning the details of Woody's life is figuring out *how* to learn about him. The list had these possibilities:

Ask Woody's children and grandchildren.
Ask our own families.
Look in newspapers.
Look in books.
Listen to the songs.
Look on the Internet.

I'm sure we will come up with many more ways to learn about Woody. In fact, my brother, Mark, just called me from Chicago to tell me that he is sending us a Woody Guthrie book and tape. Also, I heard there is a Woody Guthrie stamp at the post office! If you have any pictures, songbooks, or other resources we can borrow, please send them in. Steve is looking into the possibility of us interviewing Woody's daughter, Nora, who has helped establish the Woody Guthrie Archives in New York City. Of course, we will let you know more about this.

√ Ben's family gave our class the book *This Land Is Your Land.* The artist, Kathy Jakobsen, illustrated Woody's song. Monique just found out that Kathy Jakobsen will be at the Contemporary Folk Art Museum this Wednesday to speak to some college students. We were invited to go to the museum at 11:00. We will eat lunch in the park or in the classroom (if it's cold outside). [. . .] You are welcome to join us.

Interview

This week: Tuesday we will interview Jodi Schulson. [. . .]

Hurricane Relief

Early this week people will come to pick up clothes and food for the victims of the hurricane. Families from several classes contributed and were very generous. Thank you.

[. . .]

Family Homework—Week of October 19, 1998

❖ *Social Studies—People at Work*

Research Groups

[. . .]

People Who Make or Drive Vehicles. This group is making a "movie" about the production line (assembly line). You will get to see this movie at Curriculum Night on Wednesday. [. . .]

Families—Thanks for the books and news clippings you have sent to class to help this group with their research. If you see any car-related articles or have any good contacts we can meet, please speak or write to Karen.

Dance and Dancers. Pam's research group is still working on the dance about a Chinese folktale. The children are seeing that many of the dance steps are quite different from other dances they know or have seen. They are making their own book about the folktale.

When Pam read another Chinese folktale to the whole class on Friday, we were able to see that children in our class have a number of stereotyped ideas about Chinese people. We will discuss this more in class.

Eliana's mother, Lucy, has been able to rearrange her work schedule so that she can come to class every Thursday morning. She will be working with Pam's group on making costumes for their dance. [. . .] Thanks, Lucy.

Woody Guthrie. This group has continued their research about the Dust Bowl that was in the 1930s in Oklahoma and other Plains states. There was a terrible drought that dried up the land and prevented farmers from growing crops or raising animals. Farmers lost their jobs. People were hungry. Dust from the dried-up land blew everywhere and made it very difficult for people to live. Woody Guthrie wrote about this in his song "SO LONG, It's Been Good To Know Yuh." (John Steinbeck wrote *The Grapes of Wrath* about this topic. My son, Eric, is reading this book in high school. [. . .] There is a video of *The Grapes of Wrath* if you are not familiar with this aspect of United States history.)

Our research group completed a mural of a family loading up their truck with all their belongings and heading off to the West to find new jobs. [. . .]

Doing Research

Probably the most important aspect of our research is not the facts we are learning, but HOW we are finding the information. Before we do any research, we have a discussion about where we can find information. So far, we have found our information in these ways:

formal interviews
books
photographs, posters, and pictures
newspaper articles
the Internet
asking people questions
records and tapes
folktales (such as the one Pam has been using with her group)
postage stamps (such as the ones of Woody Guthrie that Ben brought to school)
T-shirts (such as the one Sam's Uncle David gave us about the marathon)
trips (such as the one to see Kathy Jakobsen's paintings about *This Land Is Your Land*)

Literature

[. . .]

Pam read a wonderful Chinese folktale called *The Empty Pot*. The emperor gives everyone who wants to become the new emperor some seeds to grow. Ping's seed will not grow, so he takes an empty pot to the emperor. Everyone else brings flowerpots that are filled with flowers. Ping becomes the emperor because he was honest. The seeds the emperor had given them had been cooked and could not grow! You might want to look for this book at the library or bookstore. [. . .]

Family Homework—Week of November 2, 1998

❖ *Social Studies—People at Work*

Our first quilting bee will take place on November 6 in the classroom. The quilt will be about our study of People at Work. [. . .] If you have any scraps of cloth, please send them in. You are welcome to join us. Thanks.

Research Groups

Dance and Dancers. The children are continuing work with Pam on their dance about Tye-May. [. . .]

People Who Make or Drive Vehicles. This group is working with Karen and trying to find out who makes the rubber tires and bumpers on cars and where the rubber is from. They are making a large diorama of rubber trees and the process of rubber production. Any information about rubber production or contacts you have would be appreciated.

We had a marvelous trip to see Chelsea's dad at work on the L train. The children were thrilled when they saw Stephan's train pull into the station. We met some of Stephan's coworkers. [. . .]

We will talk this week about the importance of subway workers in New York City. Imagine New York City without subway workers. Many of you know what that's like from having experienced subway strikes in the past. Please discuss this issue with your child. Thanks to all of the parents who joined us for this trip. [. . .] I hope it was a trip the children will always remember.

⇒ For homework, please do the subway trip worksheet.

[. . .]

Woody Guthrie. My research group worked with Ivana Espinet, from Teachers College, to make a video for Nora Guthrie. The children explained how we did the research. They explained our three murals. Also, they talked directly to Nora and told her why they wanted her to come for an interview. Immediately after Nora received and saw the video on Friday, she was so delighted with it that she called MNS to find out when she could come for an interview! Bravo to the children for doing such a great job!

   √   Woody's daughter Nora will be in our room for an interview on November 10 at 10:00 A.M. You are invited. [. . .]

❖ Reading

Last week during reading, we were talking about the word *latex* (from Karen's research group). We noticed that the *x* sounds like *ks*. We made a gigantic list of words that have the sound of the *x*. The children were so excited with their observations of the different spellings, they could hardly sit. For example, we had words like *lox* and *locks*, *Chex* cereal and *checks*, *bakes*, *cakes*, *takes*, *walks*, *talks*, *wax*, *fax*, etc. Word study can be so much fun.

   ⟹   For homework please do the *x* worksheet. Have fun. [. . .]

❖ Writing Workshop

We are beginning to see children working stories and books about some of our research topics. [. . .]

Handwriting

[. . .]
We wrote a group thank-you letter to Stephan. Then children wrote individual thank-you letters to Phoebe's father. [. . .]

❖ Math

[. . .]
We noticed some lovely patterns on the tiles in the subway. We will be looking at and making patterns this week during math. We will even add our homemade patterns to our mural about the subway and Stephan.

   ⟹   For homework, please do the math worksheet (see page 178).

[. . .]

Math Worksheet

When we were in the subway last week, we saw some tiles on the walls of the subway stations. Some of the tiles had beautiful patterns using different shapes.

Look at these patterns below. Say the patterns out loud. For example, square, square, triangle, square, square, triangle.

Look for patterns in your house, on buildings, in the subway, or in the street. Even our days have patterns: wake up, eat, get ready for school, go to school, and so on.

Work with an adult to design a pattern for a wall in your dream subway station. You might want to plan your pattern on another paper and copy it here when you are ready. Or you might want to begin work with a pencil so you can make changes.

Note: The original has more work space.

Family Homework—Week of December 7, 1998

❖ *Social Studies—People at Work*

[. . .]

Research Groups

[. . .]

Dance and Dancers. This group is focusing now on African dance. They took time to look at a map of Africa to see that Africa is a continent, not a country. They saw that Africa consists of many countries. Each country has its own types of dances. In fact, within each country, there are different types of dances.

This group is working on a dance from West Africa. We will get some help with this group from a friend of Chelsea's grandmother. Eliana's mother, Lucy, will be working with Pam's group to look at cloth from different parts of Africa. If you have any kente cloth or other African fabrics, please let us borrow them for a while. [. . .]

⇒ For homework, please do the work about the map of Africa.

People Who Make or Drive Vehicles. This group is doing research about how steel is made for use in vehicles. We are looking at some of the ingredients of steel. Two ingredients are coke (made from coal) and iron ore. We started with coal. We looked at how coal was formed millions of years ago, how miners get the coal from the earth, and how coal is converted to coke in a huge oven.

Then we looked at how iron ore was formed billions of years ago on the crust of the earth. We looked at how workers mine the iron ore. This is somewhat similar to coal mining. The children saw the similarity right away.

Our research resources:

- Photographs by Earl Dotter and my father, Milton Rogovin.
- Books (many of which were brought in by Alex's mother, who is doing a tremendous amount of research for our group), pictures, and people.
- Irena, who worked in the steel industry in Bulgaria.
- Jordan Nassau's family members, who were in the coal industry in the Pittsburgh area.
- Pam's father, who is in the steel industry in Pittsburgh and sent us some samples of coal, coke, slag, and steel.
- Me. I have been to coal mines in Pennsylvania.
- We hope to hear more from Ruth's grandfather in the spring when he comes from Ireland. He has worked in the iron industry.
- We hope to hear from Ben's mother, whose relatives worked in coal mines in the Netherlands.

- Nicholas, a student in the fifth grade, has a grandfather who is from a family of steelworkers. We will interview him.

It's amazing to me to talk to people about this particular research topic. Wherever I go, I try to tell people about it. Everybody seems to know somebody who knows something about this or has some resources. [. . .] Please let us know if you have any other resources.

The children have built a coal mine in the block area. [. . .]

Later in the week we will be making our own "steel." Actually we will make Jell-O by heating the ingredients and pouring them into molds—much the way steel is made. We need a few more Jell-O molds, please. If you have any you can lend us for a few days, please send them in. Thanks. [. . .]

❖ Reading

We have begun to read our homemade book about the Nora Guthrie interview. The children began by making predictions about what words would be in the book. They thought the word *song* would be in the book. We looked at the letter *o* in *song*. It doesn't make the usual sounds like other letter *os*, For example: *bone, boat, hot, not*. This *o* says the sound "*au*" or "*aw*"—a very sad sound. We found that same *o* sound in the words *song, wrong, Hong Kong, Ping-Pong, gong*, and more.

⇒ For homework, please do the worksheet about the *o* sound. [. . .]

Family Homework—Week of January 11, 1999

❖ Social Studies—People at Work

Upcoming Interviews

[. . .]

We will interview Chris' father, Tom. He is in the construction industry. We will visit one of the buildings he is working in later in the year. [. . .]

Jan. 19, we will interview Priscilla. [. . .] Please look for Ghana on a map. [. . .]

You are welcome to join us at these interviews.

Interviews

Last Monday we interviewed Phil Batton. [. . .] Phil is a retired teacher. Every man in his family but Phil was a steelworker in the region south of Pittsburgh. Phil was injured in a football accident when he was in high school, so he couldn't work in the steel mills. Phil's father began working in 1919, around the time of a big strike of steelworkers. We talked about the conditions in the hot steel mills. Phil said that many workers were injured and many got sick from the dust. Many got pneumonia because they were exposed to the great heat from the molten iron in the blast furnaces on their fronts and to the cold from the winter air on their backs.

In his early years, Phil's father, cousins, and uncles worked seven days a week, twelve hours a day, and received only $1.00 a day. Wow. He told us how the wives sometimes brought their young children to the fence of the steel mill so the fathers could see the children while the children were still awake.

Phil told us how the workers got together to form a union so they could get better hours, better pay, and better working conditions.

We painted a mural about the steel mill. The air around our steel mill was quite polluted.

There have been a number of articles in the newspapers lately about the issue of steel imports. Phil told us that many of the steel mills in the United States were closed. The mills were moved to other countries where workers are not paid as much.

The children were fascinated by what Phil was telling us. You would have been so proud of the questions they asked and the very intelligent discussions.

- √ Please talk about this interview.
- √ Not required: Look on a map of Pennsylvania. Find Pittsburgh. Then look south of Pittsburgh for the Monongahala River, where there were many steel mills. Then find Clairton, where Phil was brought up. There were many coal mines in that same area. Talk to each other about why the steel mills and the coal mines were in the same area.

On Tuesday we interviewed Alex's mother, Irena. She had worked for a huge company from Italy that manufactures steel mills—and all of the equipment needed for producing steel. They even trained the workers in how to use this equipment. What a great coincidence. She showed us the brochures from her company. Thanks, Irena, for the interview and for working almost daily in the classroom.

Research Groups

[. . .]

People Who Make or Drive Vehicles. During the vacation, Jordan Nassau and his family were in the Pittsburgh area. They did research about the coal mines where his relatives have worked. We will get to see the photographs very soon. Thanks to Jordan and his family.

We began our research this week about how glass is made for use in vehicles. On Wednesday, we spent the whole Research Workshop asking questions and writing the questions in our journals. The children had these and other questions:

Can glass break easily?

How is glass made to fit in cars?

Can you always see through glass?

How thick is glass?

How is glass measured?

How is glass cut?

How is glass made?

The next day we made a list of ways to find answers to our questions. Did you know that glass is made from sand, limestone, and soda ash? Very often recycled glass is added to the mixture. [. . .] If you know anyone who is involved with making glass or blowing glass, please let us know.

⇒ For homework, please do the glass worksheet.

Dance and Dancers. We had the fortune of interviewing Chelsea's grandmother's friend Asadah Kirkland. Asadah started dancing at the age of thirteen. She has studied African dance. Asadah taught us a dance called the Lamban from Mali in Africa. The children from Pam's research group showed Asadah the dances they had learned from Ghana and from China. Thanks so much, Dawn, for arranging this wonderful experience. Asadah was stunned by the depth of knowledge our children had about different cultures and about dance. She commented that it was amazing to see such young children drawing connections between this and past interviews, and between social studies issues and literature. She's right! The children are terrific!

√ Please talk about this interview and look for Mali on a map. [. . .]

❖ Reading

When the children were writing about Phil and about Asadah, I noticed that so many were writing words like *tim* instead of *time*, *mad* instead of *made*, *lik* instead of *like*. We learned some "magic" we could use to make the vowel say its name instead of its sound—we added an *e* at the end of the words. Please be on the lookout for words that end with *e*—there are so many.

⇒ Please do the reading worksheet. [. . .]

Family Homework—Week of February 1, 1999

❖ Social Studies—People at Work

Research Groups

People Who Make or Drive Vehicles. We had two interviews related to this topic. On Wednesday we interviewed Ben's mother, Monique, about her grandfather, Frans, who worked in a coal mine in the Netherlands. Monique showed us a lantern that was used in the coal mine. Frans left the coal mine to do other work. Several years later, when the use of natural gas became more popular, the government of the Netherlands closed many of the coal mines it owned. The government provided money for the miners and helped retrain them for work in other industries.

On Friday we interviewed Ali's father, George, about his work, which takes him all over the world. George looks for companies that make special products. For example, he looks for companies that make things from glass that can be used for lights or lamps. He finds out more about these companies and then arranges to import their products. He has been to countries such as Greece, Poland, Czechoslovakia, Slovania, France, Italy, and more. He brought some samples for us to see. Thanks to George and Monique. [. . .]

We have had a great opportunity to expand our study of rubber, steel, and glass just by interviewing people within the MNS community (George, Monique, Phil, Raymond, and Irena). For some children, this research may go on forever. (See Glass Worksheet on p. 184.)

Dance and Dancers. Vandalyn's group was looking at *why people dance*. Please take time to discuss this issue at home. You may want to discuss dance within your own family (including dances your ancestors did) and then talk about dance in general. [. . .]

Health Care Workers and Scientists. My group looked at a great article in *Ranger Rick* magazine about sea life that is used for medical care. For example, scientists found that the sticky material in blue mussels can be used to "glue" skin together. It is now used for dental and optical work. Chitin from blue crabs is used to sew stitches. (See Reading Worksheet on p. 186.)

We also tried to answer our question, "How do health care workers keep from getting sick from exposure to patients?" We tried on rubber gloves and face masks. We looked at uniforms. If you have any health care equipment, safety equipment, or uniforms we can borrow, please send them in. Thanks.

Interviews

This week on Wednesday afternoon we will interview Aneta's mother, Jana, who is a doctor. We will interview Ruth's mother, Carmel, in a few weeks. She is a microbiologist.

⇒ For homework, please write about one health care worker you know. This could be any worker from a hospital or clinic, including

nurse
nurse's aide

Glass Worksheet

Our vehicle group is doing research about glass. We found out that the ingredients for making glass are sand, limestone, and soda ash. Sometimes recycled glass is added.

Look around your house and in the street. What do you see that is made from glass? Draw pictures and make labels for at least five things. (For extra credit draw and label ten things.)

Observe the glass carefully. What are some of the attributes that are so special about glass? One attribute of some kinds of glass is that it breaks easily—so please be very careful. Write about this on the back of the worksheet or on lined paper.

For extra credit, look in a book or magazine, find a video, ask someone, look on the Internet, or find another way to do research about glass. On the back of this worksheet or on another paper, share some of the things you learned. You are welcome to take extra time for this research. Be sure to tell where you got your information.

doctor
lab worker
transporter
worker from the medical records room
worker at a blood bank
physical therapist
psychologist, psychotherapist
medical researcher
someone from the health care workers union
or any other health care worker

It could be your own doctor or someone at your doctor's office. It could be a relative, a neighbor, or a friend. Tell as much as you can about this person. Does the person wear a uniform? What jobs do they do? If you can find out how they learned to do their job, that would be great. You don't have to put their name. You can just remember from your past experiences or even interview that person. If you don't know someone, you can just choose one health care job and do some research about that. You can make a picture or use a photograph or just write about the person.

This homework is due on Friday, Feb. 12. Please take the challenge, and do a great job on this project.

Family Homework—Week of March 8, 1999

❖ *Social Studies—People at Work*

Research Groups

[. . .]

Dance and Dancers. Vandalyn's group is learning a Cherokee dance which they will perform this week. [. . .]

Child Labor and Sweatshops. [. . .]This role-play inspired Phoebe to write a poem about child labor. We loved the poem so much that we painted a mural about it that afternoon at Center Time.

√ On March 24 we will be interviewing Ed Vargas from UNITE about the union's efforts to end child labor. [. . .]

Health Care Workers and Scientists. My group is working on a play about Elizabeth Blackwell, the first woman doctor in the United States. [. . .] You will get to see this play.

Reading Worksheet   Name _____

Our health care research group was reading in *Ranger Rick* magazine about sea life that is used for medical treatment. We read about how scientists have used the sticky part of blue mussels for a kind of glue to "glue" skin together. It is used also for repair of eyes and teeth. We read about the chitin (pronounced "kite-in") from blue crabs that is used to sew stitches during operations. We read about chemicals from the sea whip that are used to stop pain and swelling. Do you know of any medicines that are made from plants or animals? If you do, please write about that on the back of this page or on another page for extra credit.

Our research group noticed that so many of the words we used in our discussion were homophones. If you look in the paragraphs above, you will see several homophones. Circle *blue, read, for, sew, know, write, sea, mussels, eye, we, pain, made, do*.

Here are the homophones that match the words you circled above. Talk about what each word means. Draw pictures of at least five of the words.

blue	blew	I	eye
for	four	we	wee (tiny)
read	red	so	sew
know	no	write	right
sea	see		
mussels (an animal)	muscles (in our body)		
pain (hurts)	pane (window)		
do	dew (drops of water)		

Write sentences for three of the homophone pairs above (six sentences). Start with capital letters. End with a period, exclamation mark, or question mark. Make lines on the back of this worksheet or use lined paper. Write neatly.

We did a role-play where someone was going to have surgery for a broken bone, but the operating room was filthy. We realized that the laundry workers and the maintenance workers are just as important in a hospital as the doctors and nurses.

Our trip to Local 1199 was successful. We had the opportunity to meet Leonora and Bruce, who are involved in making sure that hospitals follow all health and safety rules. Bruce told us that he got involved when he was working at a hospital that didn't provide rubber gloves for the workers in the laundry. One day, the workers stopped working and demanded that the hospital provide gloves. They worked with Local 1199. The workers won. We met several other workers and learned about their jobs. Thanks to these family members who joined us. [. . .]

Interview

On Thursday we interviewed Robert Snyder, who wrote *Transit Talk*. If you had been at this interview you would have been so proud of the children. Their questions and comments were just fantastic.

The children have done so much research and conducted so many interviews that they are very skilled at drawing connections between interviews, between interview topics and their research, between interview topics and their own lives, and between interview topics and literature. We found that Robert's work is similar to what we are doing this year, learning from people by interviewing them and visiting their work.

❖ Reading

We read our homemade book, *George's Jobs*. We looked at words like *travel*, which are rather irregular. The dictionary told us that you can double the *l* or leave it single: *travelling* or *traveling*. We saw the word *over*, because George travels all over the world for his job. We will be taking a look at other words that answer the question *Where?* These are words like *over, under, around,* and *next to*.

⇒ For homework, please do the reading worksheet. [. . .]

❖ Writing Workshop

It has been a great joy to see the children writing poems, stories, and plays about our research topics. You can see their depth of interest and awareness. One of the most important things we do at our writing workshop is to find ways for children to work independently. Here are some examples:

- Using approximated spelling enables children to write words, *any* words they want and need.

- Using the word wall (wall dictionary) of our commonly used words helps them practice using a dictionary.
- Using words around the room—in our murals, on the door, in books we have read, in interview journals, on labels, etc., enables them to use the environment around them for spelling help.
- Learning editing skills they can apply without the help of an adult—putting capitals at the beginning of sentences, putting periods at the end, using quotation marks, and so on.
- Finding ways to select a new topic such as making a list of several topics, then choosing one. [. . .]

Family Homework—Week of March 22, 1999

❖ *Social Studies—People at Work*

Interview

Last Tuesday we had a wonderful interview of Paulina's father, William. William was given the polio vaccine as a baby, but he was diagnosed with polio when he was three years old. His legs were paralyzed, and he couldn't hold his head up straight. He had surgery to correct the problem with his neck. Then he had many years of physical therapy. He worked extremely hard to learn to walk again. An important part of William's physical therapy was swimming. (We talked about the fact that physical therapy is the work that Ian's father, Steve, does.)

By age fourteen, William had won twenty medals at swimming competitions. For several years William worked as a physical therapist. He worked with people who had problems similar to the ones he had as a child. During the interview, the children immediately thought of people we had interviewed or read about—Alicia, who had been a child laborer and now is helping the strawberry pickers; Wilma Rudolph, who had polio and became an Olympic gold medalist and helped get athletic scholarships for young people whose families had no money; Elizabeth Blackwell, who was the first woman doctor in the U.S. and then started her own hospital and medical school for women. It was so great that the children were able to see the similarities between these and several other people in history. You would have been thrilled to see their high level of thinking during this interview! I was!

A group of children made a two-part mural showing Wilma Rudolph running on one side and William swimming on the other. Thanks so much, William.

√ Please discuss this interview with your child. [. . .]

Research Groups

Dance and Dancers. Vandalyn has been working with this group on a mural about the Cherokee dance they performed. Also they have been looking at the contrast between instruments used with the Cherokee dance and instruments we are used to hearing in popular music. [. . .]

Artists. [. . .]They are working on sketches for their replica of a totem pole. We have been very careful to help the children understand the fact that this was an art form in a particular time period and in a particular location, so that they will not think that "all Indians make totem poles and travel in canoes." Several months ago we made a list of things the children "knew" about Native Americans. The list was totally filled with stereotypes—that Indians wore feathers, lived in te-pees, etc. Slowly, we are examining some of the stereotypes. For example, when the dance researchers were planning their mural, the children assumed that the Cherokee Indians of 150 years ago lived in tepees. After looking in books, they realized that this was not true. At that time tepees were used by the Plains Indi-ans. The children have found that *today*, many Native Americans wear the same kind of clothes we wear in New York City. The special clothes are worn at spe-cial events. [. . .]

Child Labor and Sweatshops. [. . .] On Wednesday our class will interview Ed Var-gas about the work of his union, UNITE, to end sweatshop conditions and child labor. [. . .]

Good news: Bread and Roses, the cultural group of Local 1199, has invited us to contribute our murals about child labor to an exhibition at the art gallery at the union hall (where we ate lunch). The children were so excited. [. . .]

Health Care Workers and Scientists. This research group was looking at the problem faced by health care workers and patients when they don't speak the same language. We did a role-play where Alex was the father of a child who had been injured, but he couldn't communicate with the doctor, who didn't speak Bulgarian. Aneta was the mother of a patient and the doctor couldn't speak Czech. Then I became Ash-ley's mother. I spoke in Spanish, but the workers couldn't understand me.

We tried to figure out the problems that can occur when health care workers can't find out the medical history of a patient, or can't get enough information about the patient's current problems. The children thought of various solutions—people learning each other's languages, people translating for each other, using in-terpreters. In fact, most hospitals now have a language bank, a listing of all the workers who speak languages other than English. These workers are called upon to translate when necessary. I was involved with a struggle at Columbia Presbyterian

Medical Center during the 1970s where people in the community called on the hospital to hire interpreters because so many of the patients spoke Spanish, but most of the doctors did not.

Also, we looked at the job of patient representatives, who are supposed to be advocates for the patients. [. . .]

❖ *Writing Workshop*

Last week we wrote thank-you letters to people at Local 1199 and to Evelyn.

Family Homework—Week of April 26, 1999

❖ *Social Studies—People at Work*

[. . .]
I think the children have a real strong sense of themselves as researchers.

Research Topics

Artists. [. . .] On Thursday the class interviewed Luby Mays, who is a retired teacher and a kente cloth weaver. [. . .]

Health Care Workers and Scientists. On Wednesday we interviewed Ruth's mother, Carmel. She is a medical technologist in microbiology. We took apart the word *microbiology* so we could understand its meaning. Carmel told us about the major openings through which bacteria and other germs can enter the human body. She explained how important it is for us to wash our hands, not just to put them under water, but to rub them to get the germs off.

Carmel helped us understand what happens when the doctor takes a throat culture. The doctor takes the swab, rubs our throat, and rubs the swab in a petri dish. Then microbiologists like Carmel put the petri dish in a warm incubator so that any bacteria can grow. Then they take a small sample of the bacteria and rub it on agar on another petri dish. They put various antibiotics on small pieces of special paper which they place on that petri dish. They do this so they can see which antibiotic will work best to kill the bacteria (if there is bacteria).

I think the children are much more aware now of the importance of washing themselves. Thanks so much, Carmel, for the wonderful science lesson.

√ Please discuss this interview with your child. [. . .]

Clothing Workers. It's quite amazing to see where our clothes are made. The children did a wonderful job on the surveys in the homework.

We interviewed Ed Vargas from UNITE, the clothing workers union. Jordan Nassau asked a very interesting question which I will share with you. He wanted to know how his Yankees shirt could have been made in Mexico when the Yankees team is in New York City. [. . .]

We did a role-play of a garment factory in New York City where the workers were members of UNITE. We saw how the union and the management worked to improve working conditions at the factory.

This was a very active and lively interview. [. . .]

√   Please discuss this interview with your child. [. . .]

❖ Reading

When we read our homemade book about our trip to Local 1199, we read that Bruce had been a laundry worker. We looked again at words that had *au*, *aw*, and *o* as in the word *laundry*.

⇒   For homework, please do the worksheet about *au*, *aw*, and *o*.
⇒   Read the homemade book about our interview. [. . .]

Bibliography

Works Cited and Other Professional Publications

Ayers, W., & P. Ford, ed. 1996. *City Kids, City Teachers: Reports from the Front Row*. New York: The New Press.

Banks, J. 1975. *Teaching Strategies for Ethnic Studies*. Boston: Allyn and Bacon.

Beardon, P., P. Leki, Y. Simmons, & S. Zemelman. 2000. *History Comes Home: Family Stories Across the Curriculum*. York, ME: Stenhouse.

Bigelow, B. & N. Diamond. 1988. *The Power in Our Hands: A Curriculum on the History of Work and Workers in the United States*. New York: Monthly Review Press.

Bosma, B. 1992. *Fairy Tales, Fables, Legends, and Myths: Using Folk Literature in Your Classroom*. 2d ed. New York: Teachers College Press.

Brown, C. S. 1988. *Like It Was: A Complete Guild to Writing Oral History*. New York: Teachers & Writers Collaborative.

Derman-Sparks, L. 1989. *Anti-bias Curriculum: Tools for Empowering Young Children*. Washington, D.C.: National Association for the Education of Young Children.

Devries, R., & L. Kohlberg. 1990. *Constructivist Early Education: Overview and Comparison with Other Programs*. Washington, D.C.: National Association for the Education of Young Children.

Edwards, C., L. Gandini, & G. Forman. 1998. *The Hundred Languages of Children: The Reggio Emilia Approach—Advanced Reflections*. 2d ed. Greenwich, CT: Ablex.

Fountas, I. & G. S. Pinnell. 1996. *Guided Reading: Good First Teaching for All Children*. Portsmouth, NH: Heinemann.

Gardner, H. 1978. *Frames of Mind: The Theory of Multiple Intelligences*. New York: Basic Books.

Graves, D. 2001. *The Energy to Teach*. Portsmouth, NH: Heinemann.

Harvey, S. 1998. *Nonfiction Matters: Reading, Writing, and Research in Grades 3–8*. York, ME: Stenhouse.

Harwayne, S. 1992. *Lasting Impressions*. Portsmouth, NH: Heinemann.

———. 1999. *Going Public: Priorities and Practice at the Manhattan New School*. Portsmouth, NH: Heinemann.

———. 2000. *Lifetime Guarantees: Toward Ambitious Literacy Teaching*. Portsmouth, NH: Heinemann.

———. 2001. *Writing Through Childhood*. Portsmouth, NH: Heinemann.

Heard, G. 1989. *For the Good of the Earth and Sun*. Portsmouth, NH: Heinemann.

Hindley, J. 1996. *In the Company of Children*. York, ME: Stenhouse.

Knott, A. 1999. "Fields of Shame." *American Teacher* (May/June): 14–15.

Kostelnick, M., ed. 1991. *Teaching Young Children Using Themes*. Glenview, IL: Harper Collins.

Kuklin, S. 1998. *Iqbal Masih and the Crusaders Against Child Slavery*. New York: Henry Holt.

Lewis, B. 1991. *The Kids' Guide to Social Action*. Minneapolis, MN: Free Spirit.

McIntyre, E., A. Rosebery, & N. Gonzalez. 2001. *Classroom Diversity: Connecting Curriculum to Students' Lives*. Portsmouth, NH: Heinemann.

Meier, D. 1996. *The Power of Their Ideas: Lessons for America from a Small School in Harlem*. Boston: Beacon Press.

Meier, D., J. Kozol, & J. Cohen, eds. 2000. *Will Standards Save Public Education?* Boston: Beacon Press.

Muse, D., ed. 1997. *The New Press Guide to Multicultural Resources for Young Readers: A Comprehensive Guide to Multicultural Children's Literature Featuring over 1000 Critical Book Reviews*. New York: The New Press.

Peace Child International Project. 1998. *Stand Up for Your Rights*. New York: World Book.

Peters, D. 2000. *Taking Cues from Kids*. Portsmouth, NH: Heinemann.

Pigdon, K., & M. Woolley, eds. 1993. *The BIG Picture: Integrating Children's Learning*. Portsmouth, NH: Heinemann.

Renyi, J. 1993. *Going Public: School for a Diverse Democracy*. New York: The New Press.

Rogovin, P. 1986. *Apartheid Is Wrong: A Curriculum for Young People*. 2d ed. New York: Educators Against Racism and Apartheid.

———. 1990. *Harriet Tubman and Other Plays for Young People*. Published by the author.

———. 1998a. *Classroom Interviews: A World of Learning*. Portsmouth, NH: Heinemann.

———. 1998b. *Classroom Interviews in Action*. A video. Portsmouth, NH: Heinemann.

Schniedewind, N., & E. Davidson. 1983. *Open Minds to Equality: A Sourcebook of Learning Activities to Promote Race, Sex, Class, and Age Equality*. New York: Prentice Hall.

———. 1987. *Cooperative Learning, Cooperative Lives: A Sourcebook of Learning Activities for Building a Peaceful World*. New York: Wm. C. Brown.

Shor, I., & P. Freire. 1987. *A Pedagogy for Liberation: Dialogues on Transforming Education*. New York: Bergin & Garvey.

Snyder, R. 1999. *Transit Talk: New York's Bus and Subway Workers Tell Their Stories*. Brooklyn, NY: The New York Transit Museum.

Taberski, S. 2000. *On Solid Ground: Strategies for Teaching Reading K–3*. Portsmouth, NH: Heinemann.

Turkel, S. 1974. *Working: People Talk About What They Do All Day and How They Feel About What They Do*. New York: The New Press.

Vopat, J. 1998. *More Than Bake Sales: The Resource Guide for Family Involvement in Education*. York, ME: Stenhouse.

Winston, L. 1997. *Keepsakes: Using Family Stories in Elementary Classrooms*. Portsmouth, NH: Heinemann.

Winston, L., with M. Kaplan, S. Perlstein, & R. Tietze. 2001. *Grandparents: Intergenerational Learning and Civic Renewal, K–6*. Portsmouth, NH: Heinemann.

Zaslavsky, C. 1996. *The Multicultural Math Classroom: Bringing in the World*. Portsmouth, NH: Heinemann.

———. 1998. *Math Games and Activities from Around the World*. Chicago: Chicago Review Press.

———. 1999. *Count on Your Fingers African Style*. New York: Black Butterfly Children's Books. See www.math.binghampton.edu/zaslav/cz.html

———. 2001. *Number Sense and Nonsense: Building Math Creativity and Confidence Through Number Play*. Chicago: Chicago Review Press.

Zinn, H. 1995. *A People's History of the United States: Abridged Edition*. New York: The New Press.

Works for Children

Fiction and Nonfiction

Angelou, M. & M. Courtney-Clark. 1996. *Kofi and His Magic*. Photographs by M. Courtney-Clark. New York: Clarkson Potter.

Baker, R. 1961. *The First Woman Doctor: The Story of Elizabeth Blackwell, M.D.* New York: Scholastic.

Bang, M. 1985. *The Paper Crane*. New York: Greenwillow Books.

Brown, M. W. 1982. *Goodnight Moon*. Illus. by C. Hurd. New York: Scholastic.

Bunting, E. 1989. *The Wednesday Surprise*. New York: Clarion.

———. 1994. *A Day's Work*. Illus. by R. Himler. New York: Clarion.

Burton, V. L. 1939. *Mike Mulligan and His Steam Shovel*. New York: Scholastic.

Carle, E. 1977. *The Grouchy Ladybug*. New York: Scholastic.

Cherry, L. 1992. *A River Ran Wild*. New York: Harcourt Brace Jovanovich.

Chorao, K. 1988. *Cathedral Mouse*. New York: E. P. Dutton.

Cowen-Fletcher, J. 1994. *It Takes a Village*. New York: Scholastic.

Demi. 1999. *The Empty Pot*. New York: Henry Holt.

Disalvo-Ryan, D. & M. Reisburg. 1997. *Uncle Willie and the Soup Kitchen*. New York: Mulberry Books.

Gregord, N. 1995. *How Smudge Came*. Illus. by R. Lightburn. New York: Walker.

Green, C. 1991. *Elizabeth Blackwell, First Woman Doctor*. Chicago: Children's Press.

Goldin, B. D. 1992. *Fire! The Beginning of the Labor Movement*. Illus. by J. Watling. New York: Puffin Books.

Hendershot, J. 1987. *In Coal Country*. New York: Knopf.

Hoffman, M. 1997. *Amazing Grace*. Illus. by C. Binch. New York: Dial Books.

Hoyt-Goldsmith, D. 1996. *Migrant Worker: A Boy from the Rio Grande Valley*. Photographs by L. Migdals. New York: Holiday House.

Isadora, R. 1983. *City Seen from A to Z*. New York: Mulberry Books.

Joseph, L. 1998. *Fly, Bessie, Fly*. New York: Simon and Schuster.

Keats, E. J. 1965. *John Henry, an American Legend*. New York: Scholastic.

Kent, Z. 1989. *The Story of the Triangle Factory*. New York: Children's Press.

Kroeger, M. K. & L. Borden. 1996. *Paperboy*. New York: Clarion Books.

Krull, K. 1996. *Wilma Unlimited: How Wilma Rudolph Became the World's Fastest Woman*. Illus. by D. Diaz. New York: Harcourt Brace.

Lewin, A. 1990. *Africa Is Not a Country, It's a Continent*. Milltown, NJ: Clarendon.

Lindbergh, R. 1996. *Nobody Owns the Sky: The Story of "Brave Bessie" Coleman*. Illus. by P. Paparone. Cambridge, MA: Candlewick Press.

Littlefield, H. 1996. *Fire at the Triangle Factory*. Minneapolis, MN: Carolrhoda Books.

MacDonald, M. R. 1998. *The Girl Who Wore Too Much Clothes: A Folktale from Thailand*. Thai text by S. Vathanaprida. Illus. by Y. L. Davis. Little Rock: August House Little-Folk.

McCully, E. A. 1996. *The Bobbin Girl*. New York: Penguin.

McHugh, C. 1992. *People at Work*. New York: Thompson Learning.

Maury, I. 1976. *My Mother the Mail Carrier—Mi mama la cartera*. Illus. by L. McCrady. Trans. by N. Alemany. New York City: The Feminist Press.

Pinkney, A. D. 1993. *Alvin Ailey*. Illus. by B. Pinkney. New York: Hyperion Books for Children.

Pomerantz, C. 1989. *The Chalk Doll*. Illus. by F. Lessac. New York: Lippincott.

Rudolph, M. 1992. *How a Shirt Grew in the Field*. Adapted from Russian. Illus. by E. Weihs. New York: Clarion.

Scheidl, G. M. 1993. *The Crystal Ball*. Illus. by N. Duroussy. Trans. by R. Lanning. New York: North-South Books.

Smucker, A. E. 1989. *No Star Nights*. Illus. by S. Johnson. New York: Alfred A. Knopf.

Slovbodkina, E. 1968. *Caps for Sale*. New York: Scholastic.

Steptoe, J. 1987. *Mufaro's Beautiful Daughters: An African Tale*. New York: Lothrop, Lee, & Shepard.

Taro, Y. 1987. *Crow Boy*. New York: Puffin Books.

Williams, V. B. 1982. *A Chair for My Mother*. New York: Mulberry.

———. 1983. *Something Special for Me*. New York: Mulberry.

―――. 1984. *Music, Music for Everyone*. New York: The Trumpet Club.

Ziefert, H. 1986. *A New Coat for Anna*. Illus. by A. Lobel. New York: Scholastic.

Poetry

Cullinan, B., ed. 1996. *A Jar of Tiny Stars: Poems by NCTE Award-Winning Poets*. Honesdale, PA: Boyds Mills Press.

Elledge, S. 1990. *Wider Than the Sky: Poems to Grow Up With*. New York: Harper & Row.

Giovanni, N. 1985. *Spin a Soft Black Song*. Illus. by G. Nartin. New York: Trumpet Club.

Greenfield, E. 1986. *Honey, I Love and Other Love Poems*. New York: HarperCollins.

Gunning, M. 1993. *Not a Copper Penny in Me House: Poems from the Caribbean*. Paintings by F. Lessac. Honesdale, PA: Boyds Mills Press.

―――. 1998. *Under the Breadfruit Tree: Island Poems*. Illus. by F. Vanden Broeck. Honesdale, PA: Boyds Mills Press.

Harwayne, S., ed. 1975. *Jewels: Children's Play Rhymes*. Greenvale, NY: Mondo.

Heard, G. 1998. *The Words of True Poems*. Sound recording. Portsmouth, NH: Heinemann.

Hughes, L. 1994. *The Dream Keeper and Other Poems*. New York: Scholastic.

Joseph, L. 1990. *Coconut Kind of Day*. New York: Puffin Books.

Lessac, F. 1987. *Caribbean Canvas*. Philadelphia: J. B. Lippincott.

Lewis, R. 1964. *The Moment of Wonder*. New York: Dial Press.

―――. 1968a. *Of This World: A Poet's Life in Poetry*. Photographs by H. Buttfield. Poems by Issa. New York: Dial Press.

―――. 1968b. *Out of the Earth I Sing*. New York: W. W. Norton.

Meyers, W. D. 1993. *Brown Angels*. New York: HarperCollins.

Schenk de Regniers, B., E. More, M. M. White, & J. Carr, eds. 1988. *Sing a Song of Popcorn*. New York: Scholastic.

Silverstein, S. 1974. *Where the Sidewalk Ends*. New York: HarperCollins.

―――. 1981. *A Light in the* Attic. New York: Harper and Row.

Singer, M. 1989. *Turtle in July*. New York: Macmillan.

Taberski, S., ed. 1996. *Morning, Noon, and Night*. Illus. by N. Doniger. New York: Mondo.

Photography

Bartolette, S. C. 1996. *Growing Up in Coal Country*. Boston: Houghton Mifflin.

―――. 1999. *Kids on Strike*. Boston: Houghton Mifflin.

Buirski, N. 1994. *Earth Angels: Migrant Children in America*. San Francisco: Pomegranate Artbooks.

Doherty, J. L., ed. 1981. *Women at Work: 155 Photographs by Lewis W. Hine*. New York: Dover Publications.

Dotter, E. 1998. *The Quiet Sickness: A Photographic Chronicle of Hazardous Work in America*. Fairfax, VA: American Industrial Hygiene Association.

English, B. L. 1977. *Women at Their Work*. New York: Dial Books for Young Readers.

Franklin, K. and N. McGirr, ed. 1995. *Out of the Dump*. New York: Lothrop, Lee, and Shepard.

Freedman, R. 1994. *Kids at Work: Lewis Hine and the Crusade Against Child Labor*. Photographs by L. Hine. New York: Scholastic.

Morris, A. 1998. *Work*. New York: Lothrop, Lee, and Shepard.

Newark Museum, The. 1994. *African Textiles: A Book of Postcards*. San Francisco: Pomegranate Artbooks.

Parker, D. with L. Engfer & R. Conrow. 1951. *Stolen Dreams: Portraits of Working Children*. Minneapolis, MN: Lerner.

Rogovin, M. 1995. *Triptychs: Buffalo's Lower West Side, Revisited*. New York: W. W. Norton.

Rogovin, M. & M. Frisch. 1993. *Portraits in Steel*. Ithaca, NY: Cornell University Press.

Schulke, F., ed. *Martin Luther King, Jr.: A Documentary. Montgomery to Memphis*. New York: W. W. Norton.

Videos and DVDs

Our Friend Martin. 1999. Dir. by R. Smiley & M. Maliani. New York: CBS-Fox. Videocassette. Available from video stores and online bookstores.

Mickey Mouse Goes to Haiti and the Science of Exploitation. 1995. Prod. by Crowing Rooster Arts Production. 18 min. New York: National Labor Committee.

Available from the National Labor Committee

275 7th Avenue, 15th Floor

New York, NY 10001

Phone: (212) 242-3002

Website: www.nlcnet.org

Documents a sweatshop in Haiti where Disney clothing is produced.

Modern Times. 2000. Dir. and Prod. by C. Chaplin. 103 min. Las Vegas. Image Entertainment. DVD.

Has a wonderful segment about the assembly line.

Resources for Studying Woody Guthrie

Organizations and Websites

The Woody Guthrie Foundation and Archives. 250 West 57th Street., Suite 1218. New York, NY 10107. Phone: (212) 541-6230. Website: www.woodyguthrie.org. Many of the resources in this section are available through the website.

Library of Congress. Prints and Photography Division. Washington, D.C. 20540-4731. Phone: (201) 707-0052. Websites: http://memory.loc.gov/ammen.amhome.html. http://memory.loc.gov/ammen.ndlpedu/index.html. These sites are designed for teachers. Prints and Photographs are available.

Books, Photography, Recordings, and Videos

Bell, J. & N. Guthrie. 1992. *Woody Guthrie Songbook*. New York: The Richmond Organization.

Blood, P. & A. Patterson. 1992. *Rise Up Singing: The Group Singing Songbook*. Bethlehem, PA: Sing Out.

Christensen, B. 2001. *Woody Guthrie: Poet of the People*. New York: Alfred A. Knopf.

Garman, B. 2000. *A Race of Singers*. Chapel Hill: University of North Carolina Press.

Guthrie, W. 1994. *Mail Myself to You*. Illus. by V. Rosenberry. New York: Good Year Book. Available in Spanish. A song with pictures.

———. 1995. *Seeds of Man: An Experience Lived and Dreamed*. Lincoln: University of Nebraska Press.

———. 1998. *This Land Is Your Land*. Illus. by K. Jakobsen, with contributions by P. Seeger. New York: Little Brown.

———. 2000. *Howdi Do*. Cambridge, MA: Candlewick Press. A song with pictures.

———. 2001a. *Bling, Blang*. Cambridge, MA: Candlewick Press. A song with pictures.

———. 2001b. *My Dolly*. Cambridge, MA: Candlewick Press. A song with pictures.

Guthrie, W., & M. M. Guthrie. 1992. *Woody's Grow Big Songs*. New York: HarperCollins. Book with music CD and cassette.

Guthrie, W., & P. Seeger. 1995. *Bound for Glory*. New York: New American Library.

Hurley, F. J. 1972. *Portrait of a Decade: Roy Stryker and the Development of Documentary Photography in the Thirties*. Photo ed. by R. J. Doherty. Baton Rouge: Louisiana State University Press.

Klein, J. 1999. *Woody Guthrie: A Life*. New York: Delta.

Lange, D. & P. Schuster. 1975. *An American Exodus: A Record of Human Erosion*. New York: Arno Press.

Marsh, D. & H. Leventhal, ed. 1990. *Pastures of Plenty: A Self-Portrait*. New York: Harper Collins.

Stanley, J. 1992. *Children of the Dust Bowl: The True Story of the School at Weedpatch Camp*. Illus. with photographs. New York: Crown.

Steichen, E. 1962. *The Bitter Years: Rural America as Seen By the Photographers of the Farm Security Adminstration*. New York: Museum of Modern Art.

Steinbeck, J. 1964. *The Grapes of Wrath*. Middlesex, England: Penguin Books.

Yates, J. 1995. *Woody Guthrie: An American Balladeer*. New York: Ward Hill Press.

Children's records available through Smithsonian/Folkways. Washington, D.C.
Songs to Grow On for Mother and Child SF-45036
Songs to Grow On, Vol. 1: Nursery Days SF-45036
Songs to Grow On, Vol. 3: This Land is My Land SF-7027

Other Research Study Resources

Organizations, Unions, Individuals, and Museums

American Federation of Teachers, International Affairs Department. Fax: (202) 879-4502. E-mail: iad@aft.org. The AFT has a study guide about international child labor as well as information to assist educators who are teaching about child labor. AFT has joined the Children of the Fields Campaign. This campaign supports legislative reforms and public awareness. It focuses on the exploitation of children who work in the agricultural industry.

Association of Farmworker Opportunity Program. 4350 Forth Fairfax Dr., Suite 410, Arlington, VA 22203. (703) 528-4141. Coordinating the Children of the Fields Campaign. E-mail: afop@afop.org. Website: www.afop.org.

Children's Creative Response to Conflict. Box 271, Nyack, NY 10960. Teacher resources, a newsletter, and courses.

City Lore: The New York Center for Urban Folk Culture. 72 East First Street, New York, NY 10003. Phone: (212) 529-1955. Website: www.carts.org. They have a pamphlet called "The Culture Catalog" that presents multimedia resources in folklore, history, culture, and the arts for integration across the curriculum.

Educators for Social Responsibility. 23 Garden Street, Cambridge, MA 02138. Curriculum ideas, newsletter, and resources.

Local 1199 Hospital and Health Care Employees Union. Bread and Roses Cultural Group. Phone: (212) 603-1186. Website: www.bread-and-roses.com. Educational materials about unions, art exhibitions for youth, cultural activities.

Miele Contemporary Folk Art Museum. 1086 Madison Avenue at 81st Street, New York. Phone: (212) 249-7275.

National Coalition of Educational Activists. P.O. Box 679, Rhinebeck, NY 12572. Phone: (914) 876-4590. *Rethinking Schools* newsletter has information about school reform and resources.

National Council of Teachers of English. 1111 W. Kenyon Road. Urbana, IL 61801-1096. Phone: (800) 369-6283. Website: www.ncte.org. *Primary Voices K–6.* This is a journal for elementary school teachers.

National Labor Committee. 275 7th Avenue, 15th floor. New York, NY 10001. Phone: (212) 242-3002. Website: www.nlcnet.org. Resources about efforts to end child labor and sweatshops.

Network of Educators' Committees on the Americas. P.O. Box 73038, Washington, D.C. 20056-3038. Phone: (202) 238-2379. Website: www.teachingforchange.org. *Teaching for Change: Multicultural Educational Resources.* Anti-racist and multicultural resources. Very useful curriculum guides about the Caribbean area.

Resource Center of the Americas. 317 17th Avenue, SE, Minneapolis, MN 55414-2077. Phone: (800) 452-8382. Website: www.americas.org. Catalog of resources for multicultural education. *Beyond Borders* newsletter.

Milton Rogovin. 90 Chatham Avenue, Buffalo, NY 07666. Website: www.miltonrogovin.com. Milton Rogovin is a social documentary photographer with series about coal miners, black storefront churches, workers in heavy industry, people at work and at home, and so on.

Teachers and Writers Collaborative. 5 Union Square West, New York, NY 10003-3306. Phone: (888) BOOKS-TW. *Teachers and Writers Magazine* and an extensive catalog of books and other resources.

UNITE. Union of Needletrades Industrial and Textile Employees (formerly Amalgamated Clothing Workers). 1710 Broadway, New York, NY 10019-5299. Phone: (212) 265-7000. Resources and speakers about the effort to end sweatshops and child labor.

United Farm Workers of America. AFL-CIO. c/o District Council 1708, AFSME, 75 Varick Street, 14th floor, New York, NY 10013. Phone: (212) 219-0022, ext. 108. Educational materials and speakers.

Publishers, Manufacturers, and Retailers

Bank Street Bookstore. 610 West 112th Street, New York, NY 10025. Website: http://www.bnkst.edu/bookstore. Offers a huge selection of books and other resources for any inquiry study.

Dover Publications. 31 East 2nd Street. Mineola, NY 11501-3582. The bookstore at 180 Varick Street, 9th floor, New York, has all of the Dover books. Dover publishes many books with great materials for multicultural education and inquiry studies.

Heinemann. 361 Hanover Street, Portsmouth, New Hampshire 03801. Website: www.heinemann.com. Has an extensive selection of books about education and multicultural resources.

Highsmith Press. W5527 Highway 106, P.O. Box 800, Fort Atkinson, WI 53538-0800. Phone: (800) 558-2110. Website: www.hpress.highsmith.com. Offers a huge selection of multicultural and other resources.

Malden Mills Industries, Inc. 550 Broadway, P.O. Box 809, Lawrence, MA 01842-1609. Phone: (978) 659-5146. This company makes Polartec fabrics with recycled plastics including soda bottles. They have facts sheets and a video.

Peoples African American Educational Materials. The Peoples Publishing Group, Inc. Phone: (800) 822-1080. P.O. Box 70, Rochelle Park, NJ 07662. Excellent catalog of fiction and nonfiction, maps, and other resources for multicultural education.

Syracuse Cultural Workers. P.O. Box 6367, Syracuse, NY 13217. Phone: (315) 474-1132. Website: www.syrculturalworkers.org Has an extensive catalog, *Tools for Change*, of resources for social action.

The New Press. Extensive catalog of fiction, nonfiction, and art books that are useful for teachers interested in diversity, gender, world politics, and the politics of education. 450 West 41st Street, New York, NY 10036. Phone: (212) 629-8081.

Journals and Magazines

Instructor Magazine. 73 Main Street, P.O. Box 231, Cooperstown, NY 13326. Phone: (800) 543-1284. Article by P. Rogovin. Vol. 108, No. 7.

Ranger Rick Magazine. National Wildlife Federation. 11100 Wildlife Center Drive, Reston, VA 20190-5362. Phone: (703) 438-6000.

The New Advocate, for Those Involved with Young People and Their Literature. 1502 Providence Highway, Suite 12, Norwood, MA 02062.

Index